Language and Literacy Series

Dorothy S. Strickland, FOUNDING EDITOR
Celia Genishi and Donna E. Alvermann, SERIES EDITORS

ADVISORY BOARD: Richard Allington, Kathryn Au, Bernice Cullinan,
Colette Daiute, Anne Haas Dyson, Carole Edelsky,
Shirley Brice Heath, Connie Juel, Susan Lytle, Timothy Shanahan

---

Volumes in the NCRLL Collection:
Approaches to Language and Literacy Research

JoBeth Allen and Donna E. Alvermann, EDITORS

On Narrative Inquiry:
Approaches to Language and Literacy Research
David Schaafsma and Ruth Vinz
with contributions from Sara Brock, Randi Dickson, and Nick Sousanis

On Mixed Methods:
Approaches to Language and Literacy Research
Robert Calfee and Melanie Sperling

On Teacher Inquiry:
Approaches to Language and Literacy Research
Dixie Goswami, Ceci Lewis, Marty Rutherford, and Diane Waff

On Discourse Analysis in Classrooms:
Approaches to Language and Literacy Research
David Bloome, Stephanie Power Carter, Beth Morton Christian,
Samara Madrid, Sheila Otto, Nora Shuart-Faris, and Mandy Smith,
with contributions by Susan R. Goldman and Douglas Macbeth

On Critically Conscious Research:
Approaches to Language and Literacy Research
Arlette Ingram Willis, Mary Montavon, Helena Hall,
Catherine Hunter, LaTanya Burke, and Ana Herrera

On Ethnography:
Approaches to Language and Literacy Research
Shirley Brice Heath and Brian V. Street, with Molly Mills

On Formative and Design Experiments:
Approaches to Language and Literacy Research
David Reinking and Barbara A. Bradley

On the Case:
Approaches to Language and Literacy Research
Anne Haas Dyson and Celia Genishi

On Qualitative Inquiry:
Approaches to Language and Literacy Research
George Kamberelis and Greg Dimitriadis

ON
NARRATIVE INQUIRY

Approaches to Language and Literacy Research

(AN NCRLL VOLUME)

DAVID SCHAAFSMA
RUTH VINZ

With contributions from
Sara Brock, Randi Dickson, and Nick Sousanis

Teachers College, Columbia University
New York and London

NCRLL

National Conference on
Research Language and Literacy

Published by Teachers College Press, 1234 Amsterdam Avenue, New York, NY 10027

Library of Congress Cataloging-in-Publication Data

Schaafsma, David, 1953–
    Narrative inquiry : approaches to language and literacy research / David Schaafsma and Ruth Vinz ; with contributions from Sara Brock, Randi Dickson, and Nick Sousanis.
        p. cm. — (Language and literacy series (the NCRLL collection))
        Includes bibliographical references and index.
    ISBN 978-0-8077-5203-6 (pbk. : alk. paper)
    ISBN 978-0-8077-5204-3 (hardcover : alk. paper)
    1. Language arts. 2. Reading. 3. English language—Composition and exercises. 4. Literacy. I. Vinz, Ruth. II. National Conference on Research in Language and Literacy. III. Title.
    LB1576.S3163 2011
    372.6—dc22
                                          2010051921

ISBN 978-0-8077-5203-6 (paper)
ISBN 978-0-8077-5204-3 (cloth)

Printed on acid-free paper
Manufactured in the United States of America

18 17 16 15 14 13 12 11   8 7 6 5 4 3 2 1

Contents

From the NCRLL Editors

In their preface, David Schaafsma and Ruth Vinz frame this volume on narrative inquiry by describing the narratives that language and literacy researchers write:

> Narratives told with struggle and grace—the intimacy of response, unexpected revelations, a missing detail supplied—create spaces for us to explore the complex and important work of literacy learning and teaching and the roles of language, literature, and writing in our lives.

On Narrative Inquiry embraces the struggles of theorizing, defining, conducting, and crafting narrative inquiry. The authors take us on narrative quests to exploratory spaces, introducing us to narrative scholars who engage us in philosophical and methodological discussions. Chapters by their former students Sara Brock and Randi Dickson gracefully illustrate a narrative review of research and storied interviews, respectively, which present literary alternatives to traditional dissertation sections.

And you won't believe the final chapter by Nick Sousanis! Go ahead, you can peek.

We believe that this book, like the others in the NCRLL collection, will be useful to graduate students, novice researchers, and experienced researchers who want to learn about an unfamiliar research tradition or methodology.

On Narrative Inquiry is the ninth volume in the National Conference on Research in Language and Literacy (NCRLL) collection of books published by Teachers College Press. These volumes, written by some of the most prominent researchers in the field, offer insights, information, and guidance in understanding and employing various approaches to researching language and literacy. The first eight highly acclaimed books in the "On . . ." collection are

On Qualitative Inquiry by George Kamberelis and Greg Dimitriadis (2004)

On the Case by Anne Haas Dyson and Celia Genishi (2005)

On Formative and Design Experiments by David Reinking and Barbara Bradley (2007)

On Ethnography by Shirley Brice Heath and Brian V. Street (2008)

On Critically Conscious Research by Arlette Willis, Helena Hall, Mary Montovan, Catherine Hunter, LaTanya Burke, and Ana Herrera (2008)

On Discourse Analysis in Classrooms by David Bloome, Stephanie Power Carter, Beth Morton Christian, Samara Madrid, Sheila Otto, Nora Shuart-Faris, and Mandy Smith (2008)

On Teacher Inquiry by Dixie Goswami, Ceci Lewis, Marty Rutherford, and Diane Waff (2009)

On Mixed Methods by Robert Calfee and Melanie Sperling (2010)

The "On…" books: where language and literacy researchers turn to learn. Welcome to the story.

Preface

Respect for the power of narrative—for questions derived from experiences, overheard conversations, and stories of professional lives—draws us to narrative inquiry. Inquiry begins for us when something—an event, gesture, story—calls our attention to the puzzlements contained within it. Narrative lodges within our cells. We attune our mind's eye to the stories that will inform our teaching and learning about literacy and language education, and we engage in narrative inquiry and research to illuminate the hidden, the unseen, and the neglected details of meaning as well as those that offer multiple perspectives on various aspects of learning and teaching multifarious literacies.

OPENING SPACES FOR INQUIRY

We start by puzzling out brief narrative moments. From these first glimpses, potential inquiry spaces open. Among the *narrative nuggets* gifted to us recently:

> Ninth grader Aidan says, "The best thing about summer was that I read *Catcher* four times. I never read a book more than once, and this is the first book I really liked." Just imagine the stories Aidan could tell about his reading experiences both during the summer and before. We have much to learn from Aidan about motivation, the nature of books, teaching literature, and other areas we can't even fathom.

> "In our department, there is a HUGE debate and teachers are really adamant in their positions," says Zoe, a middle school language arts teacher, "on whether our students should be allowed

to revise their writing on computers." What are the stories behind this debate? What are the stories behind the word *allowed*? Imagine what we might learn from the stories of teachers who hold such resolute positions? What might their students tell about their experiences with school-assigned and self-sponsored writing on computers? What might this group of teachers learn if they used the collection of stories to inquire for themselves?

Lara describes her attempt to produce a written account of a recorded oral narrative by one of her participants. "Today I feel like a failure! I have this uneasy feeling every time I read the transcripts. I was face-to-face with Jiao this morning, and I realized I don't trust that she can articulate her experiences with her limited English!" Imagine how a cluster of Lara's narratives on the research processes and relationship with participants might serve to further her inquiry. What experiences lead to her uneasiness? How did trying to shape an oral text into a written one lend to her realization? How might Jiao, *embodied* and face-to-face rather than distanced through recording and transcription, affect Lara's realization? What stories might Jiao tell of this experience? How do Lara's stories of this research dilemma come together with other researchers' stories?

Nathan visited a first-year teacher's classroom where silent sustained reading (SSR) is mandated for the first 20 minutes of every ELA class period. He described his experience in a student teaching seminar: "I'm looking around and seeing that students are not reading. They are quiet, but not reading. Jania rolls her pen back and forth on the desk. Rashana exaggerates a yawn every minute or two. Isaiah's book is open, but his cell phone is tucked in the pages." Nathan looks at his colleagues and says, "I remember my grandmother used to say that you can bridge a river but not an ocean. This feels like an ocean to me."

We imagine so many stories that need be told. From those who mandate SSR, to the teachers who implement the mandate, to the students who must live with the mandate daily, these narratives of experience might inform a more interpretive understanding of SSR, avoiding the relativism created by mandated practices. Imagine the narratives that could be told about bridging rivers and oceans!

These narrative nuggets are examples of what things provoke us to inquire. As literacy educators and researchers, we stand beside, behind, and within narratives that help us understand literacy as more than a subject, series of activities, curriculum, or acts of reading and writing. Narratives told with struggle and grace—the intimacy of response, unexpected revelations, a missing detail supplied—create spaces for us to explore the complex and important work of literacy learning and teaching and the roles of language, literature, and writing in our lives. In our narratives, we strive to present perspectives, invite dialogue, and nurture thoughtful interpretations about how literacy and becoming literate are not school-work but world-work.

Both of us wrote narrative dissertations and have continued to develop our uses of narrative inquiry and research. Ruth co-authored a book about writing qualitative research (Ely, Vinz, Anzul, & Downing, 1997), to be discussed at greater length in Chapter 7. Both of us experimented with multiple ways of narrating our teaching stories in various books and journals, and we also collaborated with others to help us tell our stories of teaching and learning. As we continued to develop methods of narrative inquiry in our own work, we experienced the way in which such inquiry always renews itself, the ways in which form and function enrich one another. Narrative inquiry has taught us a great deal about issues of language and literacy that we might not have learned otherwise. In this book, we invite you to consider narrative inquiry as a way of researching, learning, and reflecting.

We prefer the personal reflections of researchers in books such as Van Maanen's *Tales of the Field* (1988) and the teacher stories that both assert and embody narrative methods, such as Stock's *Dialogic Curriculum* (1995) and Paley's *Wally's Stories* (1986). But the book by David's former student and advisee, Gian Pagnucci, *Living the Narrative Life* (2004), inspired us to write this book. He reminds us just how important it is to share our thinking with others.

To You, Our Reader

As we write, we imagine you, our readers, as individuals very much like us, researchers interested in literacy education. We imagine some of you to be graduate students determining how to conduct an extended research project, one that fulfills expectations for a thesis and allows you to investigate complex issues from various perspectives. We imagine others of you to be seasoned researchers interested in extending your knowledge of narrative inquiry or planning a particular study that will involve the use of narratives of some kind. Throughout this book, you will find us making a case, as others have before us, for narrative as a fundamental way of thinking. We describe how narrative works "in relation" to the telling of a story or stories. We'll provide discussions of researchers' use of narrative inquiry to inspire you to create academic work as imaginative as it is responsible.

This book draws heavily on our experiences in writing and teaching and follows the various ways we approach narrative inquiry and story-writing in our teaching, research, and writing. Some of the examples explore various forms narrative might take and the rich sources of understanding present therein. You will find discussions on the nature of narrative and examples of narrative inquiry in teaching and learning.

Each chapter that follows will tell part of the story of our experience with narrative as a way of inquiring and researching. The plot of this book is set down to involve you as a character in this journey. We will ask you to imagine yourself in particular acts of researching and to pause in the reading to think through and write about your research interests and ideas. In the first three chapters, we introduce and illustrate uses for and ways of conducting narrative inquiry, and provide sources on the nature of narrative and narrative research along with an overview of narrative research in language and literacy education. We extend these discussions in the remaining chapters to demonstrate and discuss how narratives are constructed, the dispositions of narrative researchers and their ways of working, and the qualities of craft in narrative inquiries. In the final chapter, we offer a provocation about future considerations for narrative inquiry.

Throughout this book, we invite you to consider narrative inquiry as a way of researching the stories lives tell, those living in us, and those that might change our lives. As Okri (1997) suggests,

> We live by stories, we also live in them. One way or another we are living the stories planted in us early or along the way, or we are also living the stories we planted—knowingly or unknowingly—in ourselves. We live stories that either give our lives meaning or negate it with meaninglessness. If we change the stories we live by, quite possibly we change our lives. (p. 46)

Acknowledgments

We thank our NCRLL series editors, JoBeth Allen and Donna Alvermann, for their insightful critiques and for encouraging us to experiment with layers of narratives as each written page opened new "what if" possibilities. Our reviewers—Patti Stock, Gian Pagnucci, Susan Lytle, Jie Park, and Jessica Whitelaw—went to extraordinary lengths to offer breathtakingly detailed suggestions on how to sharpen our discussions. We thank the supportive staff at TC Press, including Meg Lemke, who directed the enterprise, and Shannon Waite, who helped with the final stages of editing and book production. To all of you—we hope you see your handiwork stitched into the pages of this book.

To contributing authors Sara Brock, Randi Dickson, and Nick Sousanis, we are grateful and enriched by your stories. We asked Randi, our friend and associate editor for *English Education*, to join us in revising the manuscript and to contribute two chapters. On one occasion, when the three of us were together, Randi exclaimed, "We have to go to bed! It's 2 A.M.! We're not kids anymore!" And we laughed, delighted about the great gift of working together again. We, who are all theoretically retirement age, seemed revived by our passionate engagement with this collaboration.

To all our students—the shaping of this text has much to do with you. Your names and stories, from our nearly 80 combined years of classroom experience, are too many to list. But please know that you carried us to further understanding of narrative through your stories and perspectives. As Bakhtin teaches us, our ideas are never quite our own; they are shaped by rich conversations with others.

To our families we offer our final thanks. Ruth's grandmother and both of our mothers tempted us to imagine the power of stories and encouraged us to become storytellers, too. Their stories reside in the nested stories of our families as narratives of living and longing continue to be shared at dinner tables, holidays, and bedtimes. Here is our wish to David's family—Tara, Sam, Ben, Harry, Hank, and Lyra—and to Ruth's family—Warren, Trace, Jason, Stacie, Katie, James, Samantha, Tobias, Aidan, and Helena: May life bring you a rich abundance of narratives to learn with and through. You sweeten the world. Just remember: A story is like a breeze, waiting for wind to carry it on to someplace else. Take up the stories and move them along!

CHAPTER 1

Why Does Narrative Matter?

Nautical charts tell sailors where to beware of Scylla and Charybdis, how to read the stories of tides, and what a perfect storm might bring. Myths are the narratives of human chartings, too, the navigation and voyages of longing and desire and curiosity and power. Narratives of experience and of the imagination are the voyages of interpretation and analysis and unmaking. As Hardy (1968) suggested, "We dream in narrative, daydream in narrative, remember, anticipate, hope, despair, believe, doubt, plan, revise, criticize, construct, gossip, learn, hate and love by narrative" (p. 5). How does all this apply to narrative research in education?

Researchers in education who gravitate toward narrative inquiry are inherently interested in details, complexities, contexts, and stories of human experiences of learning and teaching. Narratives have the potential to provide complex explanations of student and teacher identities, to shed light on issues of social justice, or to reveal contradictions in practice. Some researchers are interested in story because it resists simple answers; some, because it sheds light on veiled issues that more regularized methods of research overlook. Narratives often reveal what has remained unsaid, what has been unspeakable. It reveals the importance of context, reflexivity, difference, and multiple identities and perspectives. Narrative inquiry helps us to see more carefully and completely. It compels us to care about people's lives in all their complexity and often moves us to action.

Whether you are an experienced narrative researcher or just beginning your journey, there will be many questions that continue to tantalize. Why are narratives researched? What are the potential

1

purposes in doing so? What does narrative research ask and expect of researchers, participants, and audiences? How might narrative be used to gather, interpret, or analyze data?

If inquiry through narrative is one of our basic human activities, how and why must we teach it, how do we research with and from it, and what characteristics does narrative inquiry take in written forms? As researchers who have grappled with these questions for many years in our own teaching and scholarship, we know there are no easy or straightforward answers. However, throughout this book, we hope to help you learn what narrative inquiry is, and to share some of what we have discovered on our own journeys through the narrative labyrinth.

What Is the Research in Narrative Inquiry?

In education, Clandinin and Connelly (1990) coined the term *narrative inquiry* to describe the potential and the role of storytelling in educational experience. Methods of analysis and critique are hard to come by, but the sources of narratives (curriculum materials, articles, presentations, anecdotes, gossip, and other artifacts) construct and represent meaning in the daily lives of educators. Narrative has the potential to present complexities and ways of acknowledging the influence of experience and culture on human learning and knowledge construction. They identify this research as "a way of life" in a type of work where researchers' and participants' stories "intermesh." It is key to trust the uncertainty and tentativeness of this work. "In narrative thinking, interpretations of events can always be otherwise. There is a sense of tentativeness, usually expressed as a kind of uncertainty, about events' meaning" (p. 31).

While we acknowledge that uncertainty is part of narrative processes, our many discussions on narrative have helped us tease out at least a starting point. We define *narrative* in its broadest sense—an account, tale, interview with narrator/s; artifact, object, or action with inherent narrative; co-constructed narratives—all containing a story or stories. In narrative research, then, form and function work reciprocally. Narratives have *narrators* or re-narrators—those who relate events, describe, question, tell, and show.

During the past 2 decades, narrative inquiry has gained acceptance in many fields, but particularly in education, where terms like *narrative, narratize, narrator, narrative inquiry,* and *storying* are defined variously. Because these terms are laden with meaning and are resistant to simple, consistent definitions, we invite you to come to understand them through examples and illustrations in this book. Our hope is that you will develop rich conceptual understandings of the vocabulary of narrative inquirers, not textbook-entry definitions. We have chosen to compose this book as a variety of narratives to illustrate some of the many possible ways that researchers use narrative to conduct inquiries. One question we hope to address is, "What is the research in narrative inquiry?" Finding the stories that you might want to tell (or those that compel you to tell them!) and then choosing among the various narrating strategies we will address in Chapter 7 to help you craft them, are only the first steps in narrative research processes. Narrative nuggets, such as those posed in the Preface, might nudge you to question further, to tell other stories, or to formalize a research plan. Stories are often the beginning of the inquiry. What can be learned from narrating or reading them? Research grows out of the telling, questioning, and rendering of narratives. What further questions are the stories provoking? We will consider these issues further in this chapter.

Tandem Tellings: Constructing Narratives for Inquiry

Narrative strategies give shape to the telling. To *narrate,* then, is to do more than "give" an account or "tell" a story. The verb *narrate* suggests shaping through strategies such as repetition, intensity, linkage, magnification, tensions, and/or interruptions. The verb, *narratize,* suggests strategies of shaping that situate and reveal—within and outside the rendering of the text—the hand of the researcher/writer, context/history, and all the supporting constructions. The authorial presence is made visible in the markings of the text and in the crafting and shaping of the experiences.

In the next section we'll look at one way you might start the process, by having both researcher and participant do tandem tellings of classroom events.

A Demonstration: A Teaching/Learning Dilemma

Rochelle is in her fourth year of teaching in a school with a transitory population and high absentee rates. Her records show, averaging the first 3 years, that approximately 25.5% of her original class roster remained the same from the beginning to the end of the year. The remaining 74.5% averaged a stay of 1 to 4 months, with approximately 30% of this group staying less than a month. This tells one story of Rochelle's teaching experiences.

Take a moment before reading on to play out a narrative of what these statistics might mean to an English classroom. Imagine for a moment how the comings and goings of these adolescents might influence how a curriculum is designed, how lessons or units are taught, and the interpersonal relationships that may develop in the classroom. With these narratives you create swirling in your head, let's take a look at a couple of classroom moments through Rochelle's and Ruth's tandem tellings. Ruth has been invited by Rochelle to help her better understand how to work with her ninth-grade students, as what Rochelle considers to be sound teaching practices have not been working.

During Rochelle's teacher preparation program, she solidified her already strong beliefs that social networks augment student learning and motivation. She incorporated into her student teaching her own high school and liberal arts college experiences with collaborative project-based learning. She believed that students would benefit from small-group activities where they made decisions, solved problems, and demonstrated their learning. For her, reading was a social process where students worked to share ideas and learned from one another and the text.

Her first teaching job was in an urban high school where approximately 34% of the students lived in homeless shelters and moved quite frequently within the homeless shelter system. By Rochelle's fourth year, she was struggling to find ways to encourage collaborative learning with her students. This population—African American, Latino/a, Haitian, and Eastern European immigrants—was a racially and ethnically diverse group, but for many their unstable home lives provided a point of commonality in their discussions.

Rochelle was eager to be responsive to her students' needs. She realized that her beliefs about collaboration needed to bridge the needs, conditions, and interests of her students in ways she had yet to determine. As a result of Rochelle's concerns, Ruth and Rochelle each decided to write narratives of moments of difficulty in the classroom and use these as the basis for discussions and reflections on teaching and learning. The gathering of these stories, then, is the beginning of the inquiry. *Shaping* and *crafting* them into narratives for further examination becomes an important next step.

RUTH'S NARRATIVE (NOVEMBER 15, 2005)

The boy I can't name turns his left shoulder into the group. All he can say is, "Ah don't want to talk no more." He says it with the exactness that assumes everyone will believe him.

Hunter responds. "Who is you tellin'? Ah'm tellin' you is picky, picky. You don't wanna talk no more? Don't then. I has an opinion and you can tighten your lips. Ah'm inspirin' Doris!"

If the new boy hears Hunter's comment he doesn't let on. He simply stands and walks away. He can see the teacher and two or three of his classmates standing between where he is and the door that he wants to get to. He weaves and bobs.

I hear the boy let the door close hard behind him and see him walk toward the staircase. He is one of three new students that I haven't met.

Later, sitting with Rochelle, she talks through her thoughts about this class period. "This collection of near strangers meets in this room every day, new ones added and old ones leaving day in and day out. Some days there is a polite hush as they sit side by side with people they barely know and are asked to talk about important issues. "They put on their thin armor," Rochelle says, with the emphasis on the word *thin*. "Even those who have friendships outside of class don't necessarily bring those inside, and then this constant turnover just seems to make it harder to get them working together. And then we might get an uneasy truce and then new ones come—like Hector."

I learn the boy's name now. Hector. For Rochelle, the incident with Hector is a familiar one that repeats a few times in the course of any given week. "Week after week," she says. She describes how "they just explode sometimes" and admits, "I'm exhausted by this!" We sit down at a long table and look out the window in silence. By now all the students have left the room. "I keep reading that literature study should open worlds for the kids. The advice is all over the place: exposure to diversity; seeing themselves in the mirror. But I know it's more than that. Much more. The kids keep teaching me that." Rochelle looks out the window again, deep in her own thoughts.

My mind moves elsewhere in our shared space of silence. The constructions of social class, gender, sexual orientation, and race are not raised by most of these young readers, and, when they are voiced, some students state their objections to talking about any of this. We've been looking at this aspect of Rochelle's work over the past 3 months. Much of the traditionally taught literature offers these adolescents a look into worlds that normalize racial tokenism, silence gay and lesbian issues, and fail to trouble male-dominated relations or bring to the surface social issues that seem beyond resolution. What Rochelle intended originally was to develop a curriculum that would expose how the ideological and political weight of the literature causes the students to look at how the texts function as constructing sites.

I hear Rochelle's voice again through the fog of my thinking. Rochelle is saying, "These students mostly don't want to read literature that raises questions. They seem to want pleasure reading, if they want to read at all. They keep telling me that. I'm beginning to feel like I rob them of that possibility when I demand that they think about how the text works in society and on the reader to raise issues of inequality or injustices. That's when we seem to get these tensions and almost rages. It's like that is a way of deflecting the hard conversations and just escaping from them."

As Rochelle talks, I move back into my own experiences as a high school teacher. What spaces did I try to open, or did the students open spaces that I might not have noticed at the time? What resistances didn't I see? What did it mean to teach in the contexts I had in comparison with the particular challenges of Rochelle's situation? I think of these things and the thoughts attach themselves to the mesh of what Rochelle and I are trying to understand about working with these adolescents. There is so much I don't understand and can't link to my own experiences. The silences that surround these thoughts carry messages I haven't learned to read.

ROCHELLE'S NARRATIVE (NOVEMBER 15, 2005)

For the second day in a row I see the tears in Hector's eyes. He looks around as he leaves the room and blinks them away. I know he must be telling himself not to let anyone see. He just wants to keep the little streams of water from cascading off his cheeks. I wonder what he is thinking. He told me when he came here that in the school he came from, "well, the kids just turn away. Ah's an alien and won't last. Ah was so out of there." His nose glistens with beads of sweat as he says this. I think he might cry, and I shift in my chair, hoping to take the weight off the moment. I nod. "Hector, your classmates want to get to know you. Don't you think they want to get to know you for who you are?" He takes it as a sign.

"Why you askin'? A teacher's never done that before, ever. Ah don't know what they think." He smiles, expecting me to do something, but I'm not sure what or how to respond.

I shift again. In some ways it is just a fixed way of responding. I ask because I don't know what else to say. I feel he is interpreting too much from my simple question.

I remember the feeling when he said that—a tiny little knock in my heart. Just some modest success for him here, I was thinking. I think he is a good boy. But usually, he is a boy of too few words and then today he goes and says something. Today, first thing I notice is Hunter's bushy eyebrows rise and wrinkle his brow. He spits words back at Hector. I could hear them and still don't know most of what happened. I asked both boys. Here are their versions.

Hector said, "Hunter's the don't-tell-me-a-thing guy. He don't want to hear anything Ah say. We talkin' and he sayin', 'well, social services must spend plenty of time fixin' you up. You got a family of freaks on parade.' He's primin' for Doris. He not talking about *Speak*. He's talkin' for hisself and for Doris. He's drummin' me."

Hunter tells it a little differently. "Okay, so I say to Hector that he is not comin' along with us." He shakes his sweaty head.

His black-dyed hair and multiple piercings belie a gentler spirit. "He the baby whiner if I don't agree with him. He lookin' at my Doris all the time now. Lookin' to give her an answer or some-thin' else! I tryin' to talk about the book and he just makin' up a world for Doris."

Why CAN'T they just let each other in? WHY is it everything except what we are trying to read together?

The truth is, and I need to say it over and over again to my-self as a reminder. Many of these students are homeless, living in shelters or, worse yet, in ramshackle flop hotels or on the streets. What can I expect? Is the work we are doing for them here in school making any real difference? I ask these questions knowing I will not like myself much for asking or answering them. I owe my students more.

Thoughts About These Tandem Tellings: Purposes and Dimensions

Part of the work we are doing in this book is to articulate some quali-ties inherent in the construction of narrative inquiry. As we look at Ruth's and Rochelle's brief tellings, we can see moves and strategies worth noting in the crafting. Here are four dimensions that we have come to believe are meaningful. For us, narrative

1. Makes visible the puzzles of mind—framings, evidences, stances, theories, and questions—in the researcher's com-posing of the text.
2. Challenges its own questions, answers, possibilities, and theories.
3. Grapples with issues of responsibility, power, relations, and ethics as it evidences the importance of learning with others.
4. Works to redefine the products or outcomes of research.

We ask you to consider these four dimensions and trace with us how they are or aren't present in the narratives you just read. Where is too much said or left unsaid? How do the dimensions exhibited lend to purpose and meaning? In what sense can we think of narrative as "provocateur," that is, provoking new thoughts, questions, and possible explanations for the issues and situations we are trying to understand?

What we know is that Ruth frames her and Rochelle's separate narratives within a narrative, one that feels "conventional" in that it lays out histories, statistics, and beliefs by which we can begin to understand the context of the school in which Rochelle teaches and her approach to the students. Ruth is the narrator of this framing story, and through that we are introduced to one of the main characters, the other of the two narrators. We gain some sense of the difficulties Rochelle hopes to explore with Ruth. We learn contextual background on their histories as teachers, and that Rochelle hopes that reflection will help her understand how to work more effectively with her students. Less is known about Ruth's purpose, but we know she's been invited in, and we know she's an "experience from afar," a set of eyes and ears to balance Rochelle's less seasoned "experience near" ones.

What are the questions and themes that emerge from the telling of these stories? Maybe one is "rethinking collaborative work in a transitory, high-absentee classroom environment," or "the place of social democracy when the social is highly unstable," or maybe something else or several things emerge that don't fit neatly into a topic. Brief archaeologies of social relations, of social positions—the stories work "in relation" to the "data" being considered. Subjectivities—ordinarily erased or muted in the cool objectivity of traditional social science research—get highlighted here as part and parcel of the acts of telling. There's a vulnerability in the telling and in being told about—for Ruth, Rochelle, Hector—in the process of making/becoming/presenting a moment in time, as their intersecting histories echo against the walls of the stories being constructed. As we see and hear events unfolding, we also "hear" inner voices, indirect speech, and the musings of Rochelle and Ruth. We see "the puzzles made visible," (Dimension 1) and the "theories challenged" (Dimension 2) as we focus on real kids in a real classroom facing real consequences we might never know about otherwise, and we hear of these things in some detail and complexity through the two narratives (Dimensions 1–3). We work to "redefine the products or outcomes of research" (Dimension 4) as we slow down the rush to analysis and judgment. The dual narratives complicate, rather than simplify, ways of understanding the events and motivations represented in these tandem narratives.

Throughout the process, the approach that Ruth and Rochelle take is to write narratives of "moments" they can study together. Readers come into the process of sense-making. Although Ruth lacks a deeper history with these kids, she uses her senses to pay attention to details she makes come alive with rich sensory language: The boy "weaves and bobs," for instance. She works hard to replicate the speech of the students. Why? What purpose does that serve in the broader purpose of the narrative? She begins to etch the boy into our memory, to make us as interested in him as she is, and for the same reasons, to see him as she does. She listens hard to Rochelle speak of the kids' "thin armor" which reveals so much about their vulnerability and helps us understand things about the kids and about Rochelle as an observant, sensitive teacher. Ruth shows it; we feel it. In the story Ruth tells, senses matter although they cannot necessarily be trusted, and the same is true for perceptions, although the reader will judge the sense of honesty, and, in this particular version of co-construction, Rochelle is there to challenge or arbitrate.

As Ruth tells her story of the events about Hector, her mind doubles back to the 3 months they have been working to explore issues that emerge in this classroom, and these link to stories of her own teaching as her memories intermingle with observations. She attempts to contextualize embodied and embedded moments in time as she tries to capture the circumstantial quality of the field of inquiry. There's the silence here, too, in various ways, the silence of reflection, the unsaid confusions, the speechless inability to understand how to help these students learn in the ways they might best learn. It's not a triumphant story modeling successful teaching strategies for collaboration in a diverse classroom, like the ones we most often read; rather, it's a story troubling the ways such taken-for-granted strategies just don't work sometimes in certain situations. In this sense, it "challenges its own questions, answers, possibilities, and theories" (Dimension 2). Ruth even admits there's a "fog" in her thinking. What's the good of admitting that?

It's possible that many teacher readers will join her in a process they know well, moving from fog to—sometimes—the light of day. Her telling gains—not diminishes—in credibility as she admits she *doesn't know*. Ruth describes a memory of her own teaching, where there's at least a triple landscape—metatextual, textual, intertextual—that all tangles together in the readings and meanings. Tensions, winces, laughter, distractions, and these dimensions of teaching and learning are appropriately present in her telling as well. She says of the students on this day, "Their silences carry messages I haven't learned to read." The beginning of the pursuit of knowledge for Ruth in this tale is in *not* knowing, and not in the *aha!* of knowing. Narrative functions here as provocateur.

Rochelle's story reveals for us the emotional details of her and Hector's teaching and learning, beginning with Hector's tears. Hunter "spits words back at Hector." She notices "Hunter's bushy eyebrows rise and wrinkle his brow." In the manner of all good story-telling, she shows us—rather than tells us about—Hunter and Hector, whose "nose glistens with beads of sweat" in this conflict. What do such details add? Why do we need to know them in a story about a classroom conflict? We see and feel the emotional weight of events for these students. She brings us there with her description. Her tale weaves layers into Ruth's version of events and leaves us—not with answers—but with a series of questions she can't (yet? ever?) answer, questions posed to us as readers, inviting us, like she invited Ruth, to join her in helping investigate and research the questions. Rochelle and Ruth don't reduce the process of learning into cognitive compo-nents, into neat variables, because they don't exist for them in that way. Instead these narratives "make visible the puzzles of the mind" (Dimension 1).

So, we have three stories where events are related, ones that Rochelle cares about, ones that Ruth comes to care about, ones they invite us as readers to care about, ones that trouble the theories that brought Rochelle—and many of us, perhaps—into the profession. The students in this context challenge her assumptions and maybe many of ours as we read. These narratives "grapple with issues of respon-sibility, power, relations" (Dimension 3) and "challenge [their] own questions, answers, possibilities, and theories" (Dimension 2). That challenge, that provocation to our assumptions, is evoked through fa-miliar and powerful narrative strategies: repetition, intensity, linkage, tensions, interruptions. There's narrating, but there's also *narratizing*, as we doubly situate and reveal the hands of the researchers as they write of this experience. The authors are present in these tales as we read them—selves revealed and questioned, vulnerabilities exposed.

So what's the power of narrative inquiry as we have experienced it here? We see real teachers struggling to raise issues of consequence for them and their students, narrating with some intensity their *not knowing* and not striving for easy answers. They don't have the answers, but they are willing to let the narratives provoke them into looking and (re)searching again as they continue to struggle with learning how to teach.

So this is one way you might join together with others to investigate a student, a policy, a classroom. What might we learn differently, if, for example, everyone in a department meeting told a story about a student as the basis for inquiry? Rather than the usual pronouncements or "summing up" of a student's behavior ("hasn't turned in a single homework," "talks constantly when he isn't sleeping"), how might trying to narrate a particular instance in all its layered complexity begin to change the way we might "rush to judgment" and perhaps miss important nuances of a student's story? Could we invite the student to tell his or her own story of sitting in our classrooms or write a narrative imagining what and how the student might narrate classroom events in ways that challenge our assumptions, beliefs, and theories? Narrative functions to open the investigation to perhaps better serve all of us. So we invite you to find places for your own tandem tellings and to see what inquiry that opens for you.

MOVING TOWARD PURPOSE

Generally speaking, when researchers choose to investigate issues of concern to them, they formulate questions and then think about how they might best be able to gain answers to or insight into those questions. The methodologies they select to conduct their research are guided by the questions they ask. We work differently. Often, we write narratives to arrive at questions to research. Narrative inquiry is particularly useful for examining the day-to-day work of teaching and learning and in gaining multiple perspectives on the way we and others experience education. We illustrate one of these purposes in the narrative that follows, one that Ruth wrote as a response to help her better understand why she was uncomfortable when she and other teachers in a September workshop reacted with amusement when one first-year teacher indicated that his first-day assignment would be to ask students to write about what they did on their summer vacations.

Ruth writes a summer vacation narrative as a way of inquiring into the easy assumption that the assignment is not useful. At this stage in her inquiry, Ruth is gathering data by writing a summer vacation narrative. Then, the narrative was read to the teachers the next day as a way to help all of them raise questions about the summer vacation essay.

LAYERED TELLINGS:
DEMONSTRATING NARRATIVE AS PROVOCATEUR

WHAT I DID WITH MY SUMMER VACATION: A STORY IN THREE PARTS

I was excited and humbled to be asked to take a few minutes to frame your time together as we begin this new school year. Sometimes I feel like these little openers should really be given by yoga masters, those teachers who will stop time for a moment, help us catch our breath, and help us reach far past the packaged or mandated curricula that list what our students should know;beyond the steady drumbeat of testing, testing, testing; beyond this day, today, where you take deep breaths and reach out to embrace *"what might be"* this year with your students. I suppose my real task is to calm the busy-ness of the day and provoke us to reach past our common perspectives and put us in touch with the perceptual landscapes that attune us to be critical and aware and provoke us to be *restless* in our teaching.

Some of us in this room yesterday were laughing about starting our English classes with the dreaded homework assignment, "Write About What You Did on Your Summer Vacation." We all had a good chuckle, remembering the teachers who asked us to do that assignment or the times we've done it ourselves just because we weren't sure how to get started with the new school year. And, as we laughed, I thought about my own summer and the richness of stories within it that I hadn't thought about. I began thinking it isn't the assignment itself that is wrongheaded.

It's the way I came to assigning it and the stain of cynicism that closes down the possibilities of the spaces of learning the assignment might open. So, as a way of keeping me *restless in my teaching*, I went home last night and wrote this little narrative to share with you today.

Part I

Returning to the Panhandle of Idaho this past summer, I was reminded at almost every turn of Lewis and Clark who crossed the continent in 1804 and 1805. The landscape that loomed before them daily had no name and no markers. They had fallen off the edge of their maps. They learned to name for themselves. They learned, not nearly often enough, to trust the native inhabitants, to learn anew, to break their easy assumptions, and to question what they believed as "the way things are." Many of the old rules didn't apply. How disconcerting and how liberating it must be, I thought, to step one foot after another into a space of unknowing and uncertainty. They carried intuition, previous experiences, values, and beliefs that helped them read the signs of their journey. They also carried a healthy disregard for all they had been told and had learned. But, they must have carried more—the deep urge to face the new and to chart the way for themselves. The deep urge to be part of the creating.

I am reminded as I retell this moment that the map is often overdrawn for teachers and for our students in classrooms, with scripted curriculum and standards and objectives written on the board. In too many classrooms, students don't have opportunities to use (and, yes, challenge) the repertoire of texts from family lore, songs and stories, proverbs, names for places and persons, recipes, rules never spoken but known within the familiar circle of their experiences and imaginings. They are often not given many opportunities to step out into the spaces of the unknown and learn for themselves. And, walking one of those trails that Lewis and Clark had charted for all of us, I wanted to veer off their path and find my own. I want to remember this in my teaching—offering up the spaces and not the maps—not leading the trek but finding ways to be the provocateur, the "learner whisperer." And, for all of us, the challenge that is this journey of teaching: How can we open spaces for our own and students' learning and imagining?

Part II

This summer I found my old viola in my uncle's barn. The case looked like crackle paint. Inside, still wrapped in green felt the spruce belly lay exposed, gleaming the molecular quilt of its wood. The winter freezes of more than 40 years had snapped the catgut strings. The bow hairs had withered from disuse. The wood puckered around the sound hole, imitating the pursed lips of a frown as if to remind me that the song, the thing this viola had to say, had been cast off and forgotten—by me. I learned that a viola dies if not played and not noticed. If only I could bow the first stroke on the strings again . . . if only it would come alive again and sing its own song. Willing it so, the sound began to glide off the imagined strings—I could almost hear it. As if in response, the barn swallows scattered. And, I took the image in to remember something about the power of the will.

Teaching and learning are about what we "almost know"— those uncertain spaces where we have the glimmer of hunches, confusions, and, yes, of the song that isn't being sung but that we can hear in our bones. In my experience, all pleasure in learning begins with a sense of abundance—boundless curiosity, the feeling of light. A muse—like this old viola—reminds me how very generous life is when I take time to see and listen. "Hold that thought," I whisper, "for a moment." Attention and expectation hold the moment still for contemplation—for the song still in an old viola or for the one residing in an adolescent who can't seem to find the song to sing or to hear. Attention and expectation make the barn swallows scatter just as the song begins to rise.

Part III

My aunt in Moscow, Idaho, asks: "What was it like to be in New York City on September 11?" I remember that strange day but don't have the will to talk about it. Instead, a flood of emotions. "I was thinking," she said, "how that day we became part of the world's suffering." She turned 98 this past August, and I glance at her steady hand touching my arm. "When the Twin Towers fell," she continues, "it became our turn to suffer and we were stunned by images of people all over the world caught on film, celebrating in the streets. And, yet, I remember images of us in the newspaper, shouting in the streets, hugging each other, defiant after the bomb was dropped at Hiroshima."

How did we get to this place? What intricate moves must we take to learn and to teach the assets of peace rather than war? And, suddenly, with my aunt's hand on my arm, I longed to feel her arms around me again, teaching me to dance a waltz around the dining room table where we had gathered for holiday dinners. And, I took her, in my arms this time, and started to hum and to move her, ever so slowly at first, those frail bones ready to jump from the parchment skin that held in all that energy and love. And then she laughed and moved her feet, the slippers sliding on the old pine boards. I held her tight, wanting the urge to dance to linger in the air. And, so it goes. Teaching is about the urge to dance and the millions of intricate moves we take "in relation" to others.

That was my summer vacation. I hope I captured the fits and starts and inconsistencies and cluttered meaning. You had your own summer vacation. I'd urge you to consider what you cradle in your brain that is worth writing about and thinking through, and to imagine how these thoughts will inform your teaching, will invite you to re-see; re-think reified categories, words, and forms that have lost meaning, like the "Summer Vacation Essay," and have a look around. It's your journey. It's for you and your students and future students with whom you will learn. The world depends on it!

*   *   *

This piece, we think, shows how narrative can act as provocateur because the telling resides in a stitched-together boundary between the explicit and implicit, in the interstices of what is said and left unsaid, and certainly in the spaces of silence, in the assumed, in the unquestioned. One story generates further stories. Stories have meaning beyond themselves as Dyson and Genishi (2005) recommend in their discussion of case study approaches to research. To capture the fluidity, meaning-in-motion, and uncertainty is to narrate the filling up, not the boiling down and obfuscation, of life-in-the-living. Narrative researchers learn the lessons of seeing differently and probing those places and events overflowing with cluttered meaning.

An Invitation

As we said at the beginning of this chapter, we live by narrative in ways that we may not even think about. Narrative probes, takes pictures, just as summer vacation narratives have demonstrated. We even chart the seas and the heavens through narrative. For example, the Hubble telescope is taking on a similar role, sending back images that can be told or written as narratives—stories of stars growing, glowing, and dying out; narratives of black holes and strings connecting universes together into nets; planets made and unmade. Here is a recent narrative from the Hubble Web site (hubblesite.org):

> January 14, 2010: Galaxies throughout the universe are ablaze with star birth. But for a nearby, small spiral galaxy, the star-making party is almost over. Astronomers were surprised to find that star-formation activities in the outer regions of NGC 2976 have been virtually asleep because they shut down millions of years ago. The celebration is confined to a few die-hard partygoers huddled in the galaxy's inner region. The explanation, astronomers say, is that a raucous interaction with the neighboring M81 group of galaxies ignited star birth in NGC 2976. Now the star-making fun is beginning to end. With no gas left to fuel the party, more and more regions of the galaxy are taking a much-needed nap. The star-making region is now confined to about 5,000 light-years around the core.

Stop for a moment and just imagine the images, the stories of galaxies forming and dying as Hubble continues the voyage as "time machine" to *show* in narrative images, to capture the universe 500 million years ago and mark a region that is 5,000 light-years around its core. It is too much to comprehend without narrative. And, imagine the next stories unfolding as Hubble continues on the journey. Then, imagine the narratives you will have to tell as you make your voyages and inquiries into the places and spaces you hope to explore.

CHAPTER 2

Entering a Conversation on Narrative: A Knot of Many Crossings

In a knot of eight crossings, which is about the average size knot, there are 256 different "over-and-under" arrangements possible. . . . Make only one change in this "over and under" sequence and either an entirely different knot is made or no knot at all may result.

—Ashley, 1944, p. 167

The challenge for us in this chapter is to tie a series of knots that provide an overview of literature that explores the multiple conceptions, purposes, and craft in narrative approaches to research. Since the 1980s, researchers increasingly have found narrative inquiry to be a provocative method for studying issues in education, particularly in the areas of language and literacy. A discussion follows of texts and authors we have found useful in demonstrating or explaining the interpretive traditions and methodologies that inform diverse ways of thinking about narrative.

Imagine David and Ruth sitting on the floor surrounded by a stack of their 40 favorite books in various genres that have challenged or deepened their thinking about narrative inquiry. Behind them are row after row of additional books that inform narrative research. Ruth leans against one of the bookcases, "Our task is to turn this undisciplined tangle into a manageable knot."

"Ruth, let's emphasize the idea that we invite our readers to participate in an ongoing conversation about conceptions of narrative and narrative practices." Ruth turns to the computer screen and begins writing:

> The ongoing conversations and debates on narrative as a form
> of inquiry and research demonstrate a lack of consensus on how
> to define narrative, the data sources, the modes of investigation,
> the researchers' positionality in relation to the participants, and
> understandings of purposes and outcomes of narrative research.
> In this chapter, we tie conceptual strands of narrative theory
> with traditions in narrative research and identify key tensions
> and issues in narrative-based approaches. Then, we offer a dis-
> cussion of many of the narratives that have helped us conduct
> and craft our research projects. We hope this overview helps
> you locate your interests in the larger field and offers avenues
> for further investigation that prove interesting and productive.

David nods. "That's useful, I think, but . . . wouldn't it be more interesting if we could story all of this?"

"We have the same challenge here that puzzles anyone trying to work in narrative—space and selection." Ruth arcs her arm around the room in a sweeping gesture toward the clutter. "Our readers need to enter these narrative waters and tie their own knots of understanding. Let's take them fishing."

GOING FISHING

Weary of stale air and the smell of dust, book spine after spine with "narrative" in the titles, you gather your notes, shut down your computer, and head for lunch. Maybe it's the warm sun or the creamy penne settling in your belly, but after you leave the restaurant you feel the urge to sit on a park bench and watch the river. It's been a long morning of reading and the ideas jumble in your head. The smell of the river laces the air, and the boats reflect glimmers of sunlight. You imagine swimming out to one of those boats.

Since you are fishing for information, answers to your questions, and ideas about how to map the tides, tidepools, and riptides that will constitute your understanding of narrative inquiry, you board one of the fishing boats. You take your position at the prow, bait your hook, and trawl the high seas of narrative research and inquiry. Each "fish" you hook turns out to be a person with strong opinions about narrative work. You bring all these people together onto your metaphoric boat, and, of course, they can't resist sharing their beliefs about narrative. Remember, this must be a large boat that will not tip over as tempers flare, orators gesticulate, and the weight of uncertainty tips it starboard. No one takes the helm, and you feel the boat start to drift. You begin catching the meaning of their ideas and think that even Bakhtin's (1981) conception of heteroglossia can't steel your nerves from an overwhelming sense that the differences in belief impact how you will choose to do your research.

For a moment, you set aside your pole and examine what you have hooked. You find Clandinin and Connelly (1990) stretched out in deck chairs, talking about their work. These are familiar waters. Clandinin stresses how important it is that researchers reflect on their own identities by incorporating their research stories into the narratives. She is interrupted by Craib (2004) who points out that narrators may not recognize complexities. Narrators may stereotype experience and events or not come to terms with the struggle within themselves to distinguish the life as told from the life as lived. He reminds Connelly and Clandinin that "when I tell my story it is an 'interpretive feat,' a construction of my life. There is no simple and unproblematic record of my life" (p. 73). This conversation calls into question the *interpretive authority* not only of researchers' work with others' stories but also of researchers' storying and reflecting on their own stories.

You look out toward the river. What Clandinin said was something you had read or heard often enough that you accepted the idea as a given. Now your boat sways as you wonder whether there is any solid ground of certainty. Just as you turn back to ask a question, Lacan (1977), who had been hunkered down on the port side listening, stands and points at the group. He reminds everyone that individuals are pliable and narrated versions of reality. A person cannot repair the fragmentation and disharmony within consciousness. He raises the question of whether any telling, any language, can in fact anchor a subject's identity. The unconscious starts to look as though its origin is in the symbolic order, he tells you, and a subject's sense of a stable identity is complicated by the vicissitudes of language.

You wonder whether there is any credence in trying to tell or hear your own or others' stories. This conversation reminds you of Denzin's (1997) comments on the "crisis of representation." The phrase *crisis of interpretation* describes what you are struggling to understand. What are the ways to mediate between researcher and researched? As you are thinking about this, Clough (2002) leans in close against your left ear and whispers that you must blur distinctions "not only between form and content, but also between researcher and researched, between data and imagination; to insist, that is, that the language itself, by itself, does the work of inquiry, without recourse to the meta-languages of methodology" (p. 3).

J. Bruner (1986) challenges Lacan: "With science, we ask for some verification (or proof against falsification). In the domain of narrative . . . we ask instead that, upon reflection, the account correspond to some perspective we can imagine or 'feel' as right" (pp. 51–52). Clandinin nods, and you feel on more stable footing.

Ochberg (2003) suggests that "how we should pay attention to meaning varies from one community and one historical moment to another. To see how this is so is to restore interpretation to history" (pp. 130–131). "No one group," adds Collins (1991), "possesses the theory or methodology that allows it to discover the absolute 'truth' or, worse yet, proclaim its theories and methodologies as the universal norm evaluating other groups' experiences" (pp. 234–235). Joining Collins in speaking from the perspective of marginalized women, Mohanty (1991) and Spivak (1999) remind everyone on the boat that researchers' unexamined ethnocentrism have unintended consequences. You nod now, recognizing that, as a narrative researcher, you will devote special attention to the differing ways individuals from diverse social backgrounds construct knowledge and meaning making through narrative.

Just now, a voice coming from some distance grows louder and stronger, and it takes a moment before you see Plato reading from *Allegory of the Cave* (1992). And, you realize this allegory is a text about representation and about narrative. You are reminded that narrative has a very long history indeed, and that narratology and post-narratology form a very small place at the end of a very long timeline of narrative's history.

You feel dizzy at the remarkable variety of theoretical perspectives, definitions, methodologies, and genres. Narratives pile on top of narratives and stretch out across time, place, and cultures, as you sort through competing theories, methods, and interpretive stances. How can you feel grounded with terms, language, names, and concepts like *narratological imagination, a narrativized context,* or *a fabric of traces* washing over you? You have a boatload of informants, a cacophony of disagreements, and diverse understandings and commitments. Just how can all this information be organized into a meaningful understanding of narrative inquiry?

The choppy waters of narrative are swirling around your boat. Scylla, hard on the port bow, has at least three heads in this history of narrative theories—classicism, structuralism, and post-narratological/poststructuralism. To starboard, you see the Charybdis of uncertainty and fear, who has been snagging sailors for thousands of years. You shout your question toward the sky: "Where is the how-to book on narrative inquiry?"

Delineating Narrative Histories

The historical and philosophical background of narrative theories is too long and complex a subject to discuss in any depth in this slim volume. Although it seems artificial to separate texts into categories, we do so in order to point out different ways of conceiving narrative inquiry. We suggest you consult one or more of the following texts that we have found helpful in understanding the conceptual and contextual histories of narrative theory.

McQuillan (2000) compiles selections, ranging from Plato to Said, that provide diverse viewpoints on narrative. He includes a chronology of narrative theory in the 20th century, a glossary of narrative terms, and a very helpful bibliography. More detailed accounts of particular conceptions of narrative can be found in Cobley's *Narrative* (2001), Cohan and Shires's *Telling Stories: A Theoretical Analysis of Narrative Fiction* (1988), and Mitchell's *On Narrative* (1981). Cobley (2001) lays out the relationship among orality, literacy, and narrative, and examines various historical perspectives on the relationship between narrative and everyday life: mimesis, realism, naturalism, and postmodernism. Further, Cobley identifies some categories for consideration in multidisciplinary textual analysis of narrative. Cohan and Shires (1988) highlight how language "structures possibilities of meaning" (p. 21) and emphasize how subjectivity and ideology are created by the narratives produced and consumed within a culture. Mitchell's (1981) collection of essays reflects the debates, questions, methodological confusions, and values of narrative. Reading any combinations of the books listed here will give you a sturdier and more coherent first look at theories of narrative. There are still many details to fill in, but these sources help chart a nautical map to keep you fishing.

MOVING FROM NARRATOLOGY TO NARRATOLOGIES

Narratology is the theoretical and systematic study of narrative. The underpinnings of narratology begin with Russian formalists in the 1920s. Formalists defined systems for literature with a particular eye on narrative. Two collections provide an overview of the formalists. Erlich's *Russian Formalism* (1980) and Lemon and Reis's *Russian Formalist Criticism: Four Essays* (1965) compile essays by prominent Russian formalists. The writings of Propp (1968) and Jakobson, Pomorska, and Rudy (1990) apply structuralist principles to textual analysis. Narratology was a mainstay in literary theory by the 1960s, with French structuralists, including Genette (1983), Barthes (1977), and Todorov (1981), leading the development of the field. During the 20th century, structural theorists and literary critics developed a science of narrative structure and form. Some key theorists in this group include Bal (1997), Chatman (1980), and Levi-Strauss (1967). Booth (1983) theorizes the relationship between form and meaning in *The Rhetoric of Fiction*.

Mapping even a small field of structuralist work creates a contextual bed from which you can better understand how poststructuralist critiques destabilize conceptions of narrative and topple the "ology" of narrative from a coherent view to a more contested field of study and participation. Rimmon-Kenan's *Narrative Fiction: Contemporary*

Poetics (1983) discusses the possibility of deconstruction as a method that will enrich narratology into narratologies; she paves one of the paths toward a plurality of theorizing on narrative and takes one step toward a more postmodern perspective in narrative theory.

Postmodern and poststructural influences challenged the "scientific" authority of structuralism and shifted ways of thinking about and working with narrative. Currie's *Postmodern Narrative Theory* (1998) describes the transition from structuralist narratology to postmodern principles and practices. He writes, "From discovery to invention, from coherence to complexity, and from poetics to politics: This is the short summary of the transition that took place in narratological theory in the 1980s" (p. 2). Currie plots out paths of eclectic influences that have led to how readers, narrators, and narratives are understood today: "Narratology has changed exactly because the values of standardization have been replaced in literary studies with the values of pluralism and irreducible difference: not only difference between texts but difference between readers" (p. 14).

If postmodernists destabilize assumptions about the coherence of narrative, poststructuralists identify and reveal the complex ways in which forms, discrepancies, and pluralities in narrative lead to more nuanced understandings of the mutability of texts and discourses. In *Poststructuralism and Educational Research* (2004), Peters and Burbules analyze the significance of poststructuralism to educational inquiry. In *Educational Research Undone: The Postmodern Embrace* (1997), Stronach and MacLure discuss the postmodern problem of representation and provide commentary and thoughtful examples of alternative ways of writing and reading educational research. These two books, taken together, delineate various objects and methods of study in poststructural and postmodern conceptions of researchers and research projects.

WORKING IN THE COMPANY OF OTHERS' CONCEPTUAL UNDERSTANDINGS

Various disciplines in the human sciences have come to examine narrative not only as an *object* of study, but also as a *mode* of study to illuminate experience, thought, consciousness, and identities. In every

these traditions and approaches is *a long-term goal* for any narrative researcher. We do not claim our way is the only way to organize these differences, and we recognize that cross-pollination or outright misunderstandings create various hybrids. In what follows, we provide one way of delineating these traditions and cite narrative studies that demonstrate key distinctions in purpose, questions asked, design, methods, and researcher's role.

Many language and literacy researchers follow in the traditions of Clandinin and Connelly (1990) who conceptualize narrative inquiry based on Dewey's philosophy of experience. They emphasize ways in which teachers' narratives shape and inform their personal practical knowledge, and they highlight the value of teachers' examining their own narratives or working collaboratively with researchers and others teachers to understand their experiences. Studies by Kooy (2006), Bell (1997), Jalongo and Isenberg (1995), and Florio-Ruane (1991) provide examples of purpose, emphasis, and methods within this construct. Focus on literacy teachers' narratives abound in edited collections such as Trimmer's *Narration as Knowledge: Tales of the Teaching Life* (1997) and Meyer's *Stories from the Heart: Teachers and Students Researching Their Literacy Lives* (1996).

Sociolinguistic traditions of narrative research (Labov, 1972; Labov & Waletzky, 1967) focus on narrative analyses, structures, and rhetorical choices (Linde, 1993). Attention focuses on how narratives construct and are constructed through language. Examples range from Juzwik's (2006) examination of how a teacher's narrative performances in classroom discourse contribute to learning about the Holocaust to Belcher and Connor's (2001) and Casanave and Schecter's (1997) examination of narrative constructions within language learners' and teachers' narratives.

Narrative researchers who choose to work in sociocultural traditions may ground themselves in sociolinguistics (Hymes, 1972) or neo-Vygotskyian psychology (Vygotsky, 1978). There are distinctions in methodological approaches, but both tend to explore the appropriation and internalization of literacy and language practices as cultural processes, both individually and as part of collective and contextual community practice (Dyson, 2003; Neilsen, 1998).

Researchers focusing explicitly on power and its relations to language and literacy in the traditions of critical discourses (Bourdieu

& Passeron, 1977; Foucault, 1970; Rogers, 2004) trouble the role of literacies in the formation of gender, class, and racial-ethnic identities. Looking at processes of attribution and regulation in how literacy practices are constructed, these researchers examine discursive spaces that regulate or reproduce relations of power. In this work, literacies are ideologically defined (Gallas, 1997; Quint, 1996; Sandlin & Clark, 2009).

For each of these approaches, it is important to ask, "What is at stake in choosing to work in this way?" There is not one answer, but it is helpful to think of these approaches in terms of what you hope to accomplish through your research. What do you hope your narrative work will accomplish? What do you want to learn and understand, and why might your field of study find your understanding useful? How might narrative open the spaces for interrogating the relationship between the life lived and the life told?

DETERMINING SCOPE, DATA SOURCES, AND PURPOSES

We learned about narrative research through experimentation and by deliberately weaving together information from a variety of sources. Narrative research requires inductive and creative approaches when grappling with questions about what counts as narrative data, the suitability of particular narratives over others, and the role of researcher and participants in telling and interpreting stories. By grappling with the dilemmas by "doing" our own research and reading how other researchers work with narrative, we continue to hone our practices. We've found the process of becoming narrative researchers could be likened to any research journey—continually questioning and exploring and staying open to possibilities.

Narrative research in education often involves a remembering or representing of narratives that have been produced and collected through a variety of means. We see early examples in the work of Ashton-Warner's *Teacher* (1963), Kozol's *Death at an Early Age* (1985/1967), and other autobiographical narratives. Paley (e.g., 1986, 1990) stories the learning lives of young children. Willis and Schubert (1991) write about the relationship of curriculum to their own lives.

Other narrative researchers offer multiple perspectives on the lives of teachers, students, classrooms, and schools, considering the personal experiences in relation to cultural dimensions and social experiences. Cochran-Smith and Lytle (1992, 2009) focus on teachers' reflections on their work. Witherell and Noddings (1991) focus on how to read and write lives and educational experiences through narratives. Many narrative studies in education tell of the struggles, the resistance, and the broken silences while undermining the glorification of generalizations, the over-emphasis on mass initiatives, and the promise of finding replicable "one size fits all" practices. This research calls into question the "authority" with which educational researchers have formulated understandings of learning and teaching and the experiences of schooling in other research traditions. Many projects in narrative research in education examine individual or institutional histories and try, through personal or collective memories, to explore how institutional or professional identities are named and represented. Behar (1996) reminds us, however, that personal experiences are not intended to transport the reader with "miniature bubbles of navel-gazing, but into the enormous sea of serious social issues" (p. 14). Narrative research reports are social products that come into being within the context of specific historical, cultural, and social locations in educational settings. We produce them through social inquiry. The "what to study" should be questions, concerns, and sites of study that result from your passions and curiosities.

Narrative researchers choose narratives of their own or from teachers, students, and other stakeholders in classrooms or communities. Types of narrative research include personal narratives, autobiographies and biographies, life narratives (Josselson & Lieblich, 1993), narrative interviews, life histories, life writing, diaries and journals (Rosenwald & Ochberg, 1992; Weiner & Rosenwald, 1993), oral histories, ethnohistories (Quantz, 1992), autoethnographies (Denzin, 1989), ethnopsychology (Freeman, 1992), and popular memory (Popular Memory Group, 1982). The functions, media, and structures of narratives vary widely across time, place, and cultures. The focus of subject and methodologies will vary, so it is important to read broadly, at first, to get an idea of this. For example, Josselson and Lieblich (1993) conduct phenomenological studies using narrative methods to try to understand people's lived experiences.

The use of narrative in educational research is one way of investigating theoretical and practical problems and illuminating human actions through the study of subjectivity, experience, and culture. From various paradigms and traditions, narrative researchers illuminate the complexities of examining and understanding human experience. In this work, participants and narrators tell their perspectives of how they are made and (re)made, represented and (re)represented, in learning environments. The struggle for voice is taken up by Weis and Fine in *Beyond Silenced Voices* (1993), where they include voices of those who have been marginalized by gender, class, and race. In studies that focus on "voicing," there is attention to the idea that selves are social constructions and can be changed and (re)made.

Many narrative studies explore schooling and learning through cultural lenses—identity standpoints such as race, ethnicity, class, gender, sexuality, and disability. Some of these are explicitly framed as educational research, while others—stories in the form of memoir/ autobiography, history, life history, and fiction—shed light on the potential for narratives to teach us about educational experiences from cultural perspectives.

Memoirs of schooling and intellectual biographies that focus on issues of race/ethnicity include Gilyard (1991), Villanueva (1993), Rodriguez (2004), and Anzaldua (2007). In *On Austrian Soil: Teaching Those I Was Taught to Hate* (2005), Perl writes of the emerging sense of her Jewish identity as she teaches teachers in Austria, some of whom are the children and grandchildren of Nazis. Also, Singley (2008) features the stories of both Black and White writers confronting their personal learning histories as they confront issues of race. The range of stories, both fiction and nonfiction, about schooling provide extraordinary descriptions and details about cultural dimensions of educational experiences. Consider texts that may not come to mind initially—graphic and young adult novels and memoirs that center on race or ethnicity in the context of schooling (Alexie, 2009; Yang, 2005). In unique ways, these different forms of narrative demonstrate how narrative constructs cultural identities at the same time it works to (re)present the culture of these experiences.

Life history narratives offer detailed understanding of the lives of various cultural groups. For instance, Bertram J. Cohler and Phillip

L. Hammach (2006) examine how the life stories of three gay men from different generations construct multiple identities. This life story research project explores the interplay of social change and life writing in constructing gay sexual identity. Texts that help us understand the construction of gay and lesbian identities in the context of particular historical "moments" include Duberman's *Stonewall* (1994) and Clendinen and Nagourney's *Out for Good* (2001). D'Emilio (1998), Plummer (1995), and Shilts (1987) look at the emergence and development of gay identities from the context of broader and more varied social, cultural, and historical lenses, with attention as well to schools. Bechdel's (2007) graphic memoir on the evolution of her lesbian identity in the context of her growing recognition of her father's long hidden gay identity literally illustrates a way personal narrative can help us understand the centrality of a culture of experience.

Schmidt's *Women/Writing/Teaching* (1998) is a compilation of narratives of women writing teachers in terms of their particular histories as women (see also Casey, 1993; Middleton, 1993). Individual teaching memoirs by women about being women in schools/the academy include Grumet (1988) and Walkerdine (1991). There are numerous "cultural" texts that look at the intersections of race and gender, such as Royster's (2000) study of African American teachers teaching for social change. The long tradition of Black women's storytelling offers insights into diverse ways of thinking about sites of learning and challenges notions that schools can be normalized and regularized and still meet the needs of all students (Bell-Scott & Johnson-Bailey, 1999; Johnson-Bailey, 2000). In this tradition, Lawrence-Lightfoot (1985, 2003) and Walker (2005) have storied in depth sociological perspectives on schooling through their narratives.

Class and disability are additional cultural frames for narrative studies. Books that focus on class issues include Rose's *Lives on the Boundary* (2005), a look at Rose's own and his students' rise from the lower to middle classes through schooling; for a look at how upper class schools construct elite students, consider Khan (2010). Dews (1995) narrates stories of working-class academics. Eagleton (2003), Walkerdine (1991), and Finn (2009) narrate tales of working with working-class students. Stories of disabilities include R. O'Brien's (2004) interviews with various individuals with disabilities. Grealy's

(2003) memoir of disability, especially her struggles in school, provides rich descriptions of how school culture clashes with the cultural lives of individuals or groups (cf. Alexie, 2009).

While we have separated out and named these narratives as demonstrations of particular cultural standpoint, please know that we recognize that these same narratives portray other identity standpoints as well. The narratives can teach us much about the subtle ways in which cultural identities are constructed and constructing, and how they express and are expressed in ways that provide a window onto cultural experiences and expectations of learning and teaching.

A number of studies focus on specific populations. Farrell, Peguero, Lindsey and White (1988) examine students considered at risk of dropping out of school. Altenbaugh (1992) and Gitlin (1992), present teachers' narratives. Studies of feminist teachers include Weiler's *Women Teaching for Change* (1988; see also 1992) and Middleton's *Educating Feminists* (1993). Sterling (1984) explores women's perspectives through diaries, letters, and other writing.

Foster (1997) conducted life history interviews of Black teachers who discuss their teaching practices and educational philosophies. Henry (1998) presents narratives of five African Canadian women teachers. Their narratives present multiple contradictions about their positioning as "minority" teachers who have alternative pedagogical strategies as well as "standpoints" in North American/Western school traditions. Fordham (1988) focused on high-achieving Black students who "act White" to succeed in school. Cohen (1993) provided accounts of students' experiences, while Britzman (1991) examined lived experiences of student teachers against the normative discourses of schooling.

These inquiries conceive of teachers and students as rich sources of understanding about teaching and learning, and complicate any simple representations of them. While narratives have no easy relationship to experience, the stories told begin to help us explore life experiences as related to opinions, worldviews, contextual elements, and changing interpretations over time.

Discovering Narrative Practices for Yourself

Almost any narrative you read deeply can be useful for the purpose of figuring out the nature of narrative and for examining acts of storying experience and events. We presume you already have a project or possible projects in mind. Here are questions to consider related to your interests:

- What about narrative is compelling to you?
- Why might narrative inquiry be a meaningful way to study the topic that interest you?
- What type of narratives might you collect or construct in order to better understand your topic of interest? What might different types of narratives reveal?
- Are you interested in researching with others—students, teachers, community members—by writing narratives together, or do you want to study others' narratives?

This might be a good time to stop and write responses to some of these questions.

One way to understand narrative inquiry is to revisit the stories you most enjoy, the ones that speak to you or position you in ways to understand others' perspectives. Think about narrative at its best— how it inspires, terrifies, thrills, perplexes, or lures you toward some experience or understanding. We are constantly reading various types of narratives, including traditional and experimental novels, young adult literature, graphic novels, narrative poetry, memoirs, and narrative theory and research, to challenge our thinking about narratives' purposes and constructions.

We encourage you to think about the texts that lie stacked on your bedside table and the ones you grew up loving, and reflect on what drew you to them. What makes these successful or compelling stories? Examine how these texts embody the qualities of craft that you want to learn more about—for example, verisimilitude (J. Bruner, 1991, pp. 4–5); narrated situation (Iser, 1993, p. 167); self-reflexivity (Cunliffe, 2003, p. 988); or disappearance (Docherty, 1996). Start here—reading, naming, noticing, and jotting notes.

RETHINKING NARRATIVE AS A READER AND WRITER

We find it useful to read, view, and talk about texts that do not fit into the traditional views of narrative since we believe that almost all writing is part of a narrative arc. Films that work against traditional narrative structures include Linklater's (1991) *Slackers*, where the wandering, apparently formless structure seems to echo the aimlessness of the title characters. Consider Reggio's (1982) *Koyaanisqatsi: Life out of Balance*, where the nonnarrated, apparently random relationship of sequences seems to speak to ecological disorder.

We encourage you to read from works such as Auster's (2001) edited collection of stories, tales submitted to Auster from ordinary people, not professional writers. Or, take a look at Drooker's rich and (almost) wordless graphic novel *Blood Song: A Silent Ballad* (2002), which can be read as usefully back to front as the other way around.

Simultaneously with the reading, take time to explore—through writing experimental narrative of your own—the essence of narrative, captured in a few dozen words. What are the complexities, the fluid views of the traditional story grammar that readers know and expect? How do the surface fluctuations, the ruptures, and collision create other versions of understood experience or perspectives? Which spaces are opened and which are closed off by these attempts to bewilder, destabilize, and challenge the predictable?

Trust that the more you write and experiment with narrative approaches, the more you learn the effects of various strategies. We have provided an array of resources in earlier sections that ground you in narrative approaches. These sources are less about *defining* narrative than *exploring* narrative, borrowing what you like as a reader for what you need as a writer.

Coming Ashore: For Now

Whether you are writing a review of literature about narrative research or writing a narrative about your teaching experiences, someone else's teaching experience, or some related educational issue *using* the literature in conversation with your story, take time to dwell in the moments of discovery. Read and write and invent the ways that best suit the stories you need to tell.

As we have emphasized throughout this chapter, it is important to read broadly and deeply. Understand the debates in the field and read about the conflicted terrain of theoretical perspectives as well as disciplinary and interdisciplinary ones that inform various approaches to narrative research. Study narrative texts closely and acquaint yourself with the purposes, questions, and modes of examination. Notice the resources of language and device used by those who write narratives well.

Our final recommendation is that you write *in narrative* about this journey through the literature. Honor the voices around and within you. In a review of literature, move beyond summary sentences and lists of texts and dates related to your topic. In narrative, each text is rooted in an image and each image leads to others. Your method of composition (i.e., narrative) matches your *recollections of reading* the texts rather than summarizing them. Tell the stories of your reading. Trust the journey through the precarious details and serpentine pathways that the reading experience takes you. And remember, one change in this "over and under" sequence can produce different narrative results. It is in the narration of your reading experiences that the knot of many crossings is told, as we will see in the next chapter.

CHAPTER 3

To Perceive Absence:
Storying a Research Journey

SARA BROCK

This chapter stories a "literature review" in ways we didn't demonstrate in the previous chapter. Sara reads the literature she is reviewing through the "screen" of her life in this double-visioned journey. Reviews of literature often are structured around this question: What is the academic scholarship in the field and how does it connect to my proposed academic scholarship? While not dismissing this way of framing as useful, we believe that reading through our lives, our bodies, and our stories provides more meaningful contexts for understanding the ways reading can work with the purposes of our scholarly work.

Our baby turned one just as I began drafting this essay. She waddled ahead of us on the cobblestones in the park. She fed herself chicken and carrots, but mostly insisted on more strawberries (in baby sign language, fingers of both hands touching, "more!"). She got into climbing, pointing, and shouting words: "duck!" (for everything with wings and feathers, even pigeons and peacocks); "sock!" (for everything that goes on feet, even my flip-flops and her daddy's boots); and "dog!" (for everything with fur, even cats and squirrels).

We went crazy—as new parents do—with cameras, cassette tapes, videos, notebooks. I even kept a tiny sketchbook, quick gesture drawings, each a version of "baby in repose"—my scribbles searching for the fold in her thigh, the dimples on the back of her hand, the roll of her cheek sinking into the hand-stitched blanket. Meanwhile, whenever possible, I read, about other (more scholarly) kinds of data gathering, perhaps not altogether different from my own, as a new mother. Heading to the park, I tucked Ruth Behar into the diaper bag, carried my baby in a sling, and when she fell asleep, we all sat down together on a bench, in the shade of an elm tree. I stacked Jerome Bruner, Bob Fecho, and Deborah Hicks in my "nursing nook" (a folding tray beside the arm of our mini-sofa), next to the burp cloth and a tall glass of water. *Eating on the Street* and *Teaching Through the Storm* rested on a windowsill beside our futon bed and I would grab them, whenever I lay down with my baby, to help her sink into a deeper slumber. Sometimes I would look forward to rainy mornings, because the drops beating on the window panes would lull my baby, letting me cover an extra chapter or two, staying in bed, reading while resting my palm on her belly, feeling the rise and fall of her tiny lungs with each breath.

Then, perhaps like a researcher after 12 months of feverish data collection, I found myself wanting to tell a story. I had an urge to write her a letter—one she could open years hence, when she'd grown up to be someone, the reader I couldn't yet know. I wanted to go from the birth—a 48-hour labor, followed by an emergency C-section, a respiratory crisis, and a week of tearfully watching my 7-pound daughter wrestle with nose tubes and IVs in an NICU incubator—to the birthday picnic under a giant oak tree in Central Park. I wanted to take the cassette spools, the shoebox of unsorted photos, the wacky sideways videos and the lined notebooks filled with scribbled sleeping faces, and bring them all together into something that she would understand. And, I would want her to trust that everything that I wrote was true.

Much as I might hesitate to place myself alongside the scholars I recently had read and admired, arriving at the end of Year 1, I began wondering whether we had something in common. I had to consider: Which story of all possible stories did I want to tell? How, from this jumble of raw data and ever-morphing memory, did I choose? Once I'd started writing, how did I fit the pieces together?

Determining Sites of Studies
and Parameters of Stories

Maybe I'm jumping ahead of myself. I found a story ("data") in the baby that sleeps in my lap as I write, but where do the scholarly researchers go for their narratives? And what leads them there? How do they hunt for stories—gather, fish, or mine for them? In my reading, I've encountered scholars who leave their universities to become visitors, observers, and witnesses; others stay in their own classrooms for practitioner inquiry; still others create a more intimate context, working with just one or a few participants who may be or become close friends. Dwelling in a more solitary space, an inner-world, there are also some researchers who make their memories their research site, inquiring into the stories of their own lives.

Traveling between home and classroom, Hicks (2002) followed Laurie and Jake from kindergarten to second grade. In her study for *Reading Lives*, she was concerned with the tensions between middle-class schools and working-class families, looking at how these tensions affect children's entry into literacy. Laurie enters kindergarten "bubbly and enthusiastic," and quickly acquires "good girl" behavior like sitting quietly and raising her hand on cue. But in first grade, forced to follow a prescribed reading progression, she runs into trouble, because the readings seem to become too difficult too quickly. Each month she slips further behind the level where the districtwide program says she should be. A diagnosis of attention deficit disorder complicates her struggles, and the medication sometimes makes it difficult for her to participate in classroom activities at all.

Laurie's classmate, Jake, enters kindergarten with a passion for NASCAR, boats, and firefighters. At home, Hicks observes Jake working alongside his father on carpentry projects, where he precociously wields an electric power saw. In kindergarten he gravitates toward the "centers" that allow him to work with his hands—the puzzles center, or the center where "he can gear up Fireman Dan with firefighting paraphernalia" (p. 100). In the first-grade classroom, however, Jake started to have angry outbursts. His progress did not meet the standards of the district-mandated program, and he started to tune out during whole-class activities, such as choral reading. Both children "began to feel like outsiders in their own classroom," and through narrative, Hicks tries to understand this estrangement.

In another study of early literacy, Gallas (2001) gathers stories of her first-grade students engaged in fanciful play—she watches the tellers of magic frog stories, the collectors of insects and their egg cases, the dancers who move like menacing lions. In her study, she explores the nature of imagination, and looks for connections between imagination and literacy. Her starting point is the story of Denzel, who cannot immerse himself in stories read aloud (he tends to fidget or daydream during story time). Gallas initially assumed that he simply lacked imagination, until one afternoon at recess, he gleefully shouted across the field: "Look, Karen, I'm running like Jell-O!" This memorable line became the title of her article.

Inspired by Denzel, Gallas began her study of the elusive topic of imagination by keeping a journal of her own mind's activity. Later, she watched Emily crawling in the mud with bugs, and Joe devoting hours to painting a dinosaur portrait—in so doing, she tried to locate some of the links between such imaginative activities and the acquisition of new discourses.

Writing from his own teaching context, a summer literacy program for middle school children in Detroit, Schaafsma (1993) probes a single explosive staff meeting. The topic of disagreement became the title of his book, *Eating on the Street*. Some students did just that— ate their brown-bag lunches on the street—when the class was taking a field trip.

What, a reader might ask, as Schaafsma does, have table manners got to do with literacy? As he reports, each teacher's version of what happened reveals intricate webs of values and beliefs that help readers appreciate how "eating on the street" became such a complicated and divisive issue among the staff members.

In the second part of his study, Schaafsma interviews the same colleagues about one student in their program, Dora. Some teachers believed her writing was remarkable; some deemed it passable; some thought that their editing suggestions had led to improvements in her work; others wondered whether the editing took something away. These stories about Dora add a layer to the stories about eating on the street, revealing some subtle (and surprising) continuities in the ways the participants talk about sandwich etiquette and writing.

"Writing out of the Unexpected" also brings together four speakers' perspectives on a single incident, but in this case the speakers belong to a team working with student-inmates at the Rikers Island jail in New York City. The researchers—Gordon, McKibbin, Vasudevan, and Vinz (2007)—worked with a small group of students and their teachers in the context of a project culminating in the publication of these students' oral histories. Three of the researchers (Gordon, McKibbin, and Vasudevan) visited Rikers regularly to facilitate the recording and editing of the oral history transcripts. In the midst of this work, something happened that these researchers found shocking. One of the students, Jermaine, slipped into an eerie kind of reminiscence, recalling his own brutal actions (jumping a Chinese take-out delivery man) with apparent glee.

In this article, each narrator tells the story from a distinct perching place in the research landscape. As an advisor to the project, Vinz listens attentively in her campus office to what the other team members report back to her. Gordon and Vasuduvan sit eye-to-eye with Jermaine as he brings forth these violent moments from his past; and McKibben travels forward in time, accompanying Jermaine's voice-on-the-page into a new school context, witnessing unforeseen responses there. What these four researchers share is an explicit commitment to exploring issues that arise in their work through stories.

While many literacy researchers visit schools to observe, or write from their current teaching contexts, others engage in interviews, inviting participants to recall events that transpired many years ago. In her dissertation, *Confirming Testimonies*, Dickson (1999) collected stories that spanned decades, as she compiled life histories of three veteran teachers—Mona, Sue, and Grace—who collectively had 120 years of teaching experience to share. In this study, even the potentially dry "statement of research questions" becomes a narrative, as Dickson shares the process of forming and refining the questions that helped her work move forward. She explains that three questions led her to the study: "What makes a great teacher? What would the participants say makes them great? And how much of that can be transmitted through formal teacher training?" (p. 59). However, as her project progressed, she found that her participants "led her to a much broader field of inquiry" (p. 60). Ultimately, her interviews with Mona, Sue, and Grace generated a new set of questions: "What is the nature of learning, for both students and teachers? What does it mean 'to teach'? How do our teaching lives and our lives outside of school intersect, diverge, reflect, and/or enhance each other?" (p. 60). At the beginning of her chapter about Mona, Dickson, believing that nothing on the page or in the data matched Mona's presence, shared her struggle to find a way to render this person who had made such a deep impression on her.

For me, it has been helpful and inspiring to read, beyond the field of education, the work of anthropologists who experimented with narrative possibilities, while crossing oceans and continents to find their stories. Wolf (1992) flew to a rice-farming village in Taiwan; Behar (1994) drove from Michigan to Mexico; and Taussig (2004) sailed upstream to a volatile region in Colombia, where gold miners and coca farmers cross paths. Brown (1991) took the subway from Manhattan to Brooklyn, where she interviewed a Haitian-born *vodou* priestess. In their ethnographic narratives, these anthropologists explore issues of political power, gender, and class in their field contexts. At the same time, they examine their own practices of crossing cultural borders to collect other people's stories and describe the challenges in refashioning these stories for their readers who are most often English-speaking scholars.

FOCUSING ON THEORY–STORY RELATIONSHIPS

In my past year of reading, between mashing yams and soaking bibs, I've noticed that narrative researchers have many different ways of talking about the role of theory in their work. Some seem to anticipate an aversion to theory on their readers' part. Admittedly, as a novice in narrative research, I haven't entirely overcome my fear that theory will ruin the stories I want to write—rob them of spontaneity, or bludgeon them into some painful and awkward condition. What kind of theories could inform my story about my baby's first year, written as a kind of love letter to her that she can read 20 or 30 years hence? I cringe at the question. Suddenly, I feel robbed of the intimacy that I want to have with my story—and with my reader.

Yet, even as I harbored these anxieties about theory, I turned to Bakhtin in a moment of distress and confusion. When I was bombarded by unsolicited advice—storms of discourse about babies, from many cultures and subcultures—Bakhtin let me vent all my frustrations (and offer them up as a paper for a doctoral seminar). With his ideas of heteroglossic language and dialogized utterances in mind, I jotted down all the insults, flattery, instructions, and random bits of baby lore that came my way in a single afternoon. I collected the words of my neighbors, two frowning señoras, disappointed that my baby would not grace them with a smile. I noted the "ooh, big brown eyes" compliment of our piano-bar-singer neighbor. I quoted our babysitter quoting her Psych 101 professor on the stages of infant development. I clipped phrases from Irish folktales about changelings, including recipes for boiled eggshell potions. And, of course, I let my child have the last word—to the extent that I could transcribe her babble. With Bakhtin by my side, the barrage of judgment-loaded words evolved from a curiosity into a story and a site of study.

In his teacher-research study, *Is This English?* Fecho (2003) recognizes theory as a natural part of everyday thinking: "We all posit tentative understandings of the world, test them in various ways, and use those understandings to refine our philosophy-in-process. . . . It's not a question of whether we theorize and philosophize . . . but to what extent we consciously involve ourselves in the process" (p. 43). Fecho foregoes an austere tone (which, some might say, customarily attends any mention of theory) and strikes a chord that might be called folksy. Perhaps reflecting his own confessed anti-theory bias, he humorously titles an early chapter in his book, "Some of My Best Friends Are Theorists," and within that chapter he heads one section, "Inviting Louise [into My Classroom]," and the next, "Inviting Lisa and Paolo." He also takes readers on a flight of fancy—his classroom, Room 256, becoming a "salon" with "a range of the great minds in education to dialogue about my practice. . . . Lisa Delpit, Louise Rosenblatt, and Paolo Freire . . . all sitting around kibitzing" (p. 49).

"It is the challenge of theory to help us move from the known to the unknown," writes Hicks in *Reading Lives* (2002, p. 57), citing

Marxist literary critic Raymond Williams. This notion of theory en-abling movement brings to mind the image of a garden with a trellis for pea plants to climb. Getting acquainted with the research of Hicks and a few other scholars, I find myself comparing their narratives to vines that grow along chain link fences or wooden lattices, curling and tangling as they rise. At times, the theory, like a rung or a wire, pokes out, bald, rusty, or weather-beaten. But often, it remains hid-den by leaves, tendrils, a weave of new and old stems.

Hicks's article, "Back to Oz? Or, Rethinking the Literacy in a Critical Study of Reading" (2004), seems vine-like, as the research narrative climbs and coils along its conceptual framework, built of ideas from bell hooks and James Gee. For this study, Hicks worked with fourth-grade girls in a "working poor" area she names "Lower Bond Hill." It is a place where "billows of dark grey smoke are emit-ted from a company that strips and refurbishes industrial barrels, some holding the residue of toxic waste" (p. 64). In the context of a re-medial reading program and after-school club at the local K–8 school, Hicks introduces readers to several girls, among them, Brandy, a 10-year-old who "wants both to get a GED and go to college" (p. 63) and, when asked about her future, "sees herself as a singer living on a farm with two kids" (p. 63). Crediting hooks, Hicks bases her study on the idea that "the language of literary texts can be one starting point for prying loose the dominant ideologies that saturate school culture" (p. 65). Writing about her own evolving understanding of how she might help girls like Brandy "negotiate class differences," Hicks also keeps in mind the ideas of Gee, specifically looking at reading as a "practice situated in the fabric of everyday life," while "questions about language and identity become paramount to a rich understanding of readers and reading" (p. 66).

A similar arrangement (with story climbing and curling round theory) appears in Destigter's article, "The Tesoros Project: An Experiment in Democratic Communities" (1998). Set within a larger rural high school, "Tesoros" was "a 10-week collaboration among Latino English-as-a-second-language students and their at-risk Anglo counterparts" (p. 10). The students who participated in this program were struggling in countless ways—some had patterns of truancy, some never saw their hard-working parents, others longed to return to their villages in Mexico, Guatemala, or Honduras. Destigter describes their melancholy affect at the first meeting: "Manuel slouched in his seat, digging tomato-field dirt from beneath his fingernails with a jack knife, while Susan stared silently out the window, still chewing on the sleeve of her sweatshirt" (p. 16).

As he narrates the story of Tesoros, Destigter stays close to Dewey's idea of *end-in-view*: "Understanding an idea as an end-in-view means that people should think of going through the process of working toward a desirable end as part of the end itself" (p. 15). At the outset of their first activity, in which students used writing and drawing to introduce themselves, "Angela leaned over to Claudia and whispered, 'I don't want to do this'" (p. 18). But by the end of the lesson, "the group now knew that Jaime's goal was to be a paramedic and that Lucia considered herself a pretty good ball player." It also had become clear that "nearly all of these students shared the experience of their families being uprooted by poverty" (p. 20). In other words, students opened up to one another about things that mattered to them. And because Dewey saw this kind of communication as central to the formation of democratic communities, Destigter writes, "we had taken modest steps toward enacting an end-in-view" (p. 20).

However, sometimes neither the metaphor of the salon nor the image of the vine-on-the-trellis can adequately represent the theory–story interplay. Sometimes it doesn't even make sense to see theory and story as separate entities; rather, the text is born as a single creature, exhaling tales, while harboring steely concepts in its teeth or in the marrow of its bones. In this kind of writing, the researcher lets the narrative stand on its own, apart from any explicit theoretical analysis, perhaps trusting that readers will understand how the story, in its own way, embodies theories and develops certain lines of thought. To my mind, this is a bold step—requiring confidence in one's own storytelling powers, as well as in one's readers.

In several brief chapters of *Schoolgirl Fictions*, Walkerdine (1991) interweaves scholarly essays with other kinds of texts, such as diary entries, field notes, poems, comics, and photos. For instance, in one brief excerpt from her field notes, Walkerdine writes about the "staffroom . . . full of women eating cottage cheese or grapefruit." Just a few lines printed on a stark, mostly blank page, this vivid notebook excerpt follows an in-depth scholarly article entitled "Progressive

Pedagogy and Political Struggle," in which Walkerdine analyzes the discourse of progressive education in the 1960s, arguing that "the liberation of children conceived in these terms did not mean the liberation of women" (p. 19). The passage she offers from her notebook could be said to convey a similar argument—perhaps even more forcefully than the essay.

INSCRIPTIONS OF SELF INTO STORY: NARRATORIAL PRESENCE AND ABSENCE

Many narrative researchers in education take on the complicated task of trying to render the stories of children who cannot write (or publish) their own versions of experience. For new parents, there is a similar kind of privileged storytelling—during this first tender year or two, a mother and father have opportunities to tell the stories of someone else's life, with an intimacy that no one else can match. Others might see my daughter fearlessly scale the bookshelves or scramble to the kitchen tabletop, but only I know how frightened she gets by the vacuum or the egg beaters, how fiercely she wraps her little limbs round my torso. Maybe this privileged narrative place is what helps me imagine writing such a long first-year letter to my daughter. Meanwhile, like many narrative researchers, I grapple with the question of where I fit into someone else's story, where I let myself become visible, and where I'd better let myself fade out.

In *Composing a Teaching Life*, Vinz (1996) mingles personal stories with the stories of participants in her study, a group of 11 people at various stages in their careers—student teachers, first-year teachers, and teachers with over 15 years of experience. Weaving her own teaching stories through the stories of her participants, Vinz returns to a critical moment in her first year. An outraged mother called, demanding that Vinz stop teaching *Lord of the Flies* immediately, because it was "the devil's work." Vinz responded by asking what, exactly, was so troublesome. Pressed for specifics, the parent admitted that she "hadn't exactly read the whole book" (p. 30). So Vinz ended the conversation by suggesting that the woman call back after reading the novel she was so keen to censor. But rather than holding up this incident as an illustration of her strength, being a first-year teacher

bullied by a parent, Vinz reflects, self-critically: "I was more interested in pursuing my agenda than in learning the art of negotiation"
(p. 30). Meanwhile, this story seems to speak to the new teachers who
participate in her study—who, in various ways, are "learning that
they are social beings who construct their teacher identities through
more than their own doing" (p. 21).

Vinz introduces us to a variety of memorable characters she encountered in her years as a high school teacher, such as Sam, a student
Ruth met in her 17th year of teaching, when she began to let students
design their own courses of study. Sam, whose father had died in
the Vietnam War, devoted his junior year to the literature of Vietnam
vets, and in this topic, discovered a lifelong passion, eventually going
on to compile oral histories of South Vietnamese survivors of the war.

The issue of how, as researchers, we handle the intersections
between our own lives and the lives we study is one that Behar addresses in her collection of essays, *The Vulnerable Observer* (1996). Her
earlier book, *Translated Woman* (1994) concludes with a controversial
chapter titled "Biography in the Shadows," in which she examines
some of the less obvious ways that her own life history intersects with
that of her collaborator, Esperanza. She explains that, despite their
outward differences (professor and peddler), she shares something of
Esperanza's "translated" status—the condition of being transported
across borders, delivered to a land unknown. In her closing vignette,
she writes about the moment when she gave Esperanza a copy of
the finished book, only to have Esperanza return it to her a few days
later, insisting, "No, *comadre*, you take it back" (p. 342). These closing
words reverberate with questions of who owns this research story,
who made it, and whose it is to keep and to tell.

During the interviews that led to *Translated Woman*, Behar and
Esperanza often brought their young children to the kitchen table
where they met—usually late at night—for cookies, soda, and the telling of life stories; and these scenes lingered in my mind as I climbed
the library stairs with my baby in a sling. We'd enter the dim stacks,
silent but for her babble, and the tick of the fluorescent timed lights.
As the months passed, and my daughter grew stronger, I'd set her
down on the linoleum floor beside me. She'd pull up on the shelves
as I filled my arms with books; then she'd make a game of taking
books down. The yellowing pages, some printed in unfamiliar alpha-
bets, would fan out in free fall.

Although I devoted over a year to this library work, locating narrative inquiry in the field of literacy never became a straightforward task. The sleuthing was always complicated by the fact that narrative inquiry often goes by so many other names—case study, portrait, oral history, life history, autobiography, ethnography, creative nonfiction, and so on. Often I relied on bibliographies for clues, looking up texts or authors that other people cited. Sometimes book reviews sent me in a promising direction.

During my months of searching, I developed an eye for abstracts, introductions, and the back-cover copy on books. Gradually, I accumulated a catalog of phrases that signaled wrong turns or wayward drifts in my investigation. As I grew more familiar with this kind of scholarship, I realized that books or articles that claimed to provide "a model" or "much-needed advice" were not the kind of material that I wanted to find. Nor did I need to go deep into books that set out to "define key characteristics," "detail the importance of" some current practice, or "debate the merits" of a certain proposal. At all costs, I avoided "research-based strategies" and "portraits of outstanding teachers," and stories that "highlight lessons learned." In other words, the kind of narrative inquiry I came to like most is not prescriptive, not definitive, not reductive.

I've also noticed that narrative researchers, like people working in any scholarly field, have their own ways of articulating their aims. Dyson (2002) emphasizes that stories are not prescriptions for practice; rather, they are "material to think with" (p. 18). Vinz says stories make it possible to explore territories filled with tensions, conflicts, and competing forces (Gordon, McKibbin, Vasudevan, & Vinz, 2007). Dickson mentions that some research questions necessitate multiple answers. And Schaafsma (1993), quoting Kundera (1988), reminds us that stories reveal the wisdom of uncertainty. Many narrative researchers point to the subtle-but-powerful features—nuance, complexity, texture, situatedness, attention to particulars, voice—that traditional social science research models tend to overlook or exclude. Hicks (2004) provocatively asks, "Who among us could depict our [own early] reading experiences or histories in a dispassionate language, devoid of feeling or concrete particularity?" (p. 67).

With issues of the power, identity, and agency of storytellers in mind, as well as issues of epistemology, many narrative researchers become highly attuned to the limits of their own work. Schaafsma

(1993) warns that any narrative, including his own, is always "in danger of doing violence to the Other that is its subject, simply because there are, for every inclusion, many more exclusions" (pp. xi–xii). Gallas (2001) admits that it would be "the height of hubris to claim" that she had arrived at a full understanding of her topic, "imagination" (p. 459). Cautious about the claims of their narrative work, these researchers seek to "initiate a discussion of what is not being spoken about" (p. 488) or simply "keep a conversation going" (Gordon et al., 2007, p. 351).

As my daughter moves beyond her first birthday, and I go on for months, with the work of drafting this bibliographic essay about scholarly narratives, I watch my daughter enter the world of stories. She brings me *Harold and the Purple Crayon*, pleading, "Apple! Apple!" Quickly, I turn to her favorite page, where the pajama-clad hero renders a tree, and a dragon to guard the fruit. "Grrr!" She growls back at the dragon. Then she pushes the book aside, and lifts up *Maisy Drives the Bus*. "Brrm! Brrm!" She greets the characters waiting at each stop. "Hi, Cyril! Hi, Tallulah!" And she cheers, along with her animal friends, when Eddie the elephant is able to board despite his irregular size. "Hooray!" Unconcerned about the way Maisy's bus route will end, she reaches for another favorite storybook, calling, "Peep!"—short for *Little Bo Peep*, in this version pictured as a toddler throwing stuffed sheep out of her crib. "Home! Home!" my daughter tells the wooly black lamb.

Lately I also have been witnessing the fragility of that part of the mind that lets us narrate, as I hear my father's storytelling strained by neurological disease and heavy medication. Sentences get interrupted, memories get scrambled, beginnings and endings get misplaced—scenes from one child's life get grafted onto another, so my daughter's infancy and my own get confused. On good days, visits with his granddaughter inspire him to tell stories I've never heard before, sometimes bringing back to life my own grandmother, whom I never got to know very well, or connecting the spinning wooden beads on my daughter's push-toy to centripetal force, and the invention of the steam engine.

Although my daughter is not yet telling full stories, she is beginning to utter words in ways that suggest story fragments. The other day, the morning of our first snowfall this winter, I went to the library for a few hours, while my husband and daughter took the subway to the Museum of Natural History. Together they lingered near the diorama with a polar bear, his wet maw lunging for a seal who bled a shocking red streak into the Arctic ice. When we all reunited at home later the same day, my daughter tucked her doll, Ernie, into her pink mini-stroller, and began wheeling circles around the floor.

"Where are you taking Ernie?" I asked.

"Moo-sem!" she answered, stroking Ernie's black felt hair and squeezing his round red nose. "Snow! . . . Train!" she added. From our window, we could see a few flakes in the air-shaft, swirling between brick walls.

"What will Ernie see at the museum?" I wondered.

"Stat-too!" (This word, *statue*, rhymes with *tattoo*, in her parlance.) "Po Beah!"

"Polar Bear?" I checked.

"ROAR!" She bellowed, and I pretended to run away from a scary animal.

Listening to this make-believe adventure, almost a story, I thought it suggested why I cannot resist the lure of narrative. Even in the halting voice of a 1-year-old girl, it lets us hear the screech and clatter of the subway, the scamper of toddler boots on the granite floors, the wild polar bear's raging growl—all on a single city morning, with snow falling silently through the sidewalk grates, melting on the underground tracks.

So it is with her own first story fragments that my missive to my daughter finally begins: "Snow! . . . Train! . . . Moo-sem! . . . Sta-too! . . . Po Bear! . . . ROAR!" Like many heartfelt letters—and, perhaps, many narrative research projects—this one never really reaches the end.

CHAPTER 4

Narrative Tracings: The Labyrinths and Corridors of Research Practices

A teacher describes how one of her 10th-grade students announces in class that he fears his reading of the first chapter of Morrison's *The Bluest Eye* is racist. "The whole class grows silent. I don't know what to do with this comment," the teacher's voice trails off. An eighth-grade girl details her frustration with the differences in what she is asked to write in her English class and her love of writing poetry and fiction outside of school. And, a professor researching an adult literacy program marvels at what one of his 50-year-old male participants endures twice a week just to get to the Literacy Center located on a drug-dealer-infested street.

Each of these stories offers a potential site for sustained inquiry that might lead to new understandings and perspectives about literacy education. But, the inquiry involves working out of these *first-told stories*, recognizing they contain deeper stories and glimpses into people's beliefs, assumptions, and experiences. In this chapter, we will discuss and demonstrate the constructing work of narrative inquiry, focusing on how to get the inquiry going, extend it through an examination of potential data sources, and provide a demonstration of how to create an inquiry space in which to examine episodes of storytelling by interrogating the influences and environments that mediate meaning making. We invite you to engage in your own inquiry in tandem with ours throughout this chapter.

Mindfulness in Research Planning

As we've emphasized, narratives have particular qualities and power that are useful for research projects in which the researcher wants to understand the details of why, what, and how something happens. A choice to engage in narrative inquiry arises from a profound desire to inquire into topics, phenomena, persons, events, or situations in a sustained way. Let us take you into an imaginary space and guide you through a process of contemplating your interests.

We invite you to close your eyes and let your mind wonder through a maze of possibilities. Let the corridors of your mind overflow with your research interests. Open the green door in front of you, the one marked *Preliminary*. An expansive foyer comes into view, and a man with a crinkle in his lip asks, "What is your research question?"

You cringe. "I don't really know. That's why I'm on this journey."

Nine women enter and push the man aside, "No need for research questions now. Puzzle out your interests first." The man slinks off into a darkened corridor. The women invite you to sit at a small desk in the corner. One of them hands you a black leather notebook and pen and nudges your arm. "Time to let the language loose." You sigh, take the pen, and stare at a pristine page.

First nothing, then slowly words slip back into your mind and travel down your arm and become the pen's ink. "That's it," they whisper. You notice their nine shadows become one as they float away, leaving you to muse about your research interests. Whether you write lists of topics of interest, narrative nuggets, or extended narratives of particular experiences, all are ways of honing what you want to study.

Writing as a Way of Inquiring

Writing is a way to puzzle out a situation, think through a series of events, or focus your research interests. Before you begin any formal plotting of a narrative study, take time to let the mind wander and wonder. As Flannery O'Connor (1985) reflects on her writing process, "I have to write to discover what I am doing. I don't know as well what I think until I see what I say; then I have to say it over again" (p. ix). Try to capture the thoughts lurking just under the surface.

Record nuggets and narrate incidents that matter to you. The preliminary writing will lead to research questions and foci. Through *the writing itself* many of the underlying assumptions, contexts, and insights will develop.

Narrative Elaborations

In what follows, we provide a demonstration of how one might begin the exploration through the labyrinths and corridors of a potential site for research, using one of Ruth's ongoing inquiry projects.

Here is Ruth's first narrative elaboration on this topic of inquiry.

The Boy in the Box (February 12)

I walk into this sixth-grade classroom and a refrigerator box takes center stage. Classmates form a larger square around it. The box has a door and cut-out windows. A handwritten sign on the door, "KEEP OUT!" Curtis sits at a small desk inside the box. The teacher, Judith, is moving around the room, stopping to check in with small groups. Curtis is alone in his box but is writing something on a piece of paper. Disquieting—this room with the boy in the box. No one seems outraged, troubled, or embarrassed. It is strangely—*normal.*

I make eye contact with Rosa, the student teacher. She believes I am here to "determine her fate," as she said to me on the phone. She wants Curtis out of this box when she is teaching. Her cooperating teacher, Judith, believes that Curtis needs to be in the box for his own safety and the safety of students around him. Rosa and her cooperating teacher are at an impasse. Rosa's university supervisor, Edith, doesn't know how to handle this, so I come to figure out some "resolution."

I try to get a look inside by leaning a little to the left of Judith's head when she stops to talk with him. Curtis stares intently at his teacher, pencil in hand, nodding until he catches my eye. He pulls half the window closed. Judith continues talking with him, but he has blocked my view. My stomach hurts. My mind brims over with indignation, frustration, and sadness.

Right now, my impulse is to clear the room of everyone—children, Rosa, Judith, Curtis—and tear the box, piece by piece, into very small squares that can be swept into the dustbin!

One of the central goals of narrative elaborations is to *(re)live* an experience in narrative, and to make "the moment live beyond the moment" (Riessman, 2008 p. 63). Ruth writes out the impact of a moment to *(re)see* and *(re)think* the issues, name the dilemmas, and determine the questions that emerge.

An invitation: Take an important incident within your research interests and (re)live it through narrative.

Inventories of an Inquiring Mind

Ruth's next instinct is to push herself to name the various perspectives that lead to further inquiry into this incident. Discovering the potential data is important work. Ruth sets a challenge for herself: Start by listing as many potential narratives as possible.

NOTEBOOK ENTRY (FEBRUARY 13)

1. The box is filled with Curtis's exquisite drawings. What are Curtis's stories about them?
2. Judith's stories of Curtis's involvement or lack thereof in class collaborations since Judith's curriculum is project-based with a strong component of cooperative learning? Students' versions of his participation? His view of himself as classmate?
3. Stories of how Curtis ends up "in the box."
4. Classmates' stories of experiences with Curtis.
5. Stories of the power dynamics and relations among cooperating teacher, student teacher, university, principal, supervisor, parents, and me.
6. Stories of Judith's and Rosa's preparation experiences (in the same teacher preparation program).

7. Rosa releases Curtis from the box—leaping over desks, scissors in hand, on the windowsill of this fourth-floor classroom with very old windowpanes! Narrate from my perspective.
8. Collect and layer stories of multiple perspectives from the noon meeting where Judith, Rosa, Edith, the principal (Mr. Taylor), and I meet.
9. Solicit Judith's story of her third-grade experience with a special needs student that left her feeling frightened.
10. Elicit Rosa's stories as the child of migrant workers where she felt herself the vanishing and invisible child.
11. Mr. Taylor 's story of Curtis's mother suggesting the box.
12. Edith's perspectives on student teachers as "guests in classrooms, not making waves, working within the cooperating teacher's structure."
13. Place my "I"s within the frame of this telling and delve into my own remembrances, beliefs, and reactions. How do I LISTEN and HEAR and RECEIVE the multiple viewpoints?
14. Published narratives on teaching and parenting students with special needs.
15. Narratives of schooling (policy documents, class procedures, district or state mandates) that focus on rules and regulations regarding special needs populations.
16. Film and fiction depictions of special needs students.

An Invitation: Inventory the narratives that have potential to inform your inquiry, even those lurking behind the more obvious or hiding in the shadows of context, appropriation, and silences. Begin with this question: *What are the possible narratives available for my study, and how will these challenge, contextualize, inform, and probe what I am studying?*

THE RAGGED EDGES OF NARRATIVE: LIMITED, PARTIAL, AND SINGLE VIEWPOINT

Narrative researchers must recognize the situated nature of both the substance of stories and the acts of telling stories they compile or solicit. These stories are stitched-together narrative realities that represent particular moments in time and are both performative and substantive. Knowing this, we recommend soliciting and compiling clusters of stories from each participant and multiple participants when possible. Let's take a look at what can be learned through a cluster of narratives from Rosa's accounts of her early school experiences.

Ruth begins by asking Rosa to participate in a series of interviews. In the first interview, Rosa tells a story about feeling invisible in school (referred to above in item 10).

> My family worked the fields in Oregon, Washington, and Idaho. We only stayed in any school for a few weeks. I was put in the last row and didn't have an identity or even a name. I was the quiet migrant girl. I felt like Curtis. I never talked. I wasn't asked to participate. I did my work and my very bad English kept other students away. Sometimes two or three of us from the migrant families were in my class and that helped because I didn't feel so alone. I just can't do to Curtis what teachers did to me. (2/16)

Ruth elicits another story about 3 weeks later by asking Rosa to talk more about her school experiences. Rosa focuses on one of her teachers.

> I remember one teacher, Mr. Jameson, who tried to help me make friends. He got me involved in an after-school reading club and would say, "Oh, Rosa, you are such a good reader and you and Theresa will be such good friends." But, when he asked me to read, I'd feel the sea washing through my stomach. Fear would take over and I couldn't get words out. It really hurt me because I was disappointing Mr. Jameson, and he would pat my shoulder. I had one friend and that was Mr. Jameson, and I could talk to him because he spoke Spanish. I choked on English because the words didn't feel right coming out of my mouth. I felt shy and awkward and alone. Other students stared at me and would just turn their backs and pretend I wasn't there. Mr. Jameson inspired me. I was in the class for 3 months and I read maybe 15 books, and he made me feel I was special, but I still didn't have friends. I'd walk home from school and then Mama was waiting with a

big smile and she would say, "You learn, Rosa?" And I'd say, "It was a good day, Mama," and smile to please her. (3/7)

Ruth solicits another story a few days later when she asks Rosa about her memories of other students from her early school experiences.

> The hurt of losing people caused me to put a strong fence around myself. I had one friend, Joyce, in second grade and she took me home to her house and I stayed overnight sometimes and I went blueberry picking and fishing with her family, and they liked me! They had a big house and her dad was a doctor and I was this skinny Chicano girl with only a little English. I would dream about a life in that house and pretend I was their daughter. Then, one day Papa said we were leaving. Too little time with Joyce and her family. I didn't ever want to make friends again because it hurt so much to leave. (3/10)

If we took any one of Rosa's narratives and assumed that it was "the story," we would fall short of opening an interpretive field toward understanding. As her stories demonstrate, narratives are selective and partial, born of contingency, situation, and purpose. At the same time, we shouldn't discount that Rosa's narratives contain unique content and viewpoints. If narratives are acts of composing ourselves and partial definitions of who we are, then as researchers we might ask how Rosa's three narratives work out partial tellings of her as student, friend, teacher, and daughter.

In another interview, Rosa speaks about her reasons for choosing teaching as a profession, reasons that were related to her view of Mr. Jameson and her desire to work with students who struggle to find spaces of success in school.

> I know I idealize Mr. Jameson when I'm telling you about him. He has become this HUGE symbol in my life of what I want to be as a teacher. It's become a mission of mine to treat each student as an individual. I see his face. The gestures of invitation. The pat on the shoulder. His reassuring voice. It isn't Mr. Jameson any longer. He is the image of myself as teacher personified. (3/16)

Rosa's narratives highlight how important it is for researchers to withhold easy conclusions or overlook the circumstances/contexts in which particular narratives are produced. We must *be alert* to opportunities for eliciting other, even counter, versions of stories that offer demonstrations of how narrators compose and define themselves through narratives. Rosa tells of her understandings through her narratives, but she also comes to understand something of her feelings and actions *through* her narratives.

Narrators need *spaces for telling*, opportunities that incite narrative production. Consider ways to invite participants to tell stories or create written narratives. Strive for clustered or layered narratives that keep the interpretive field open and elastic. However, more narratives do not mean infinite narratives. A researcher answers the question: What is the intended use of the narratives for my research project? Knowing that helps a researcher determine how many and the type of narratives to elicit—rearranging, limiting, including, and excluding—and depends on being able to articulate a purpose.

The secret to creating interpretive openings lies in the way your gaze runs over patterns, gaps, silences. Rosa's early school experiences bend into her perspectives on Curtis's situation. The path for Curtis cannot be expunged from Rosa's remembrances of Mr. Jameson and her desire to be *part of* Joyce's family as "the skinny Chicano girl." These separate building blocks of narrative moments, like parts of speech, are in working affinity with one another.

Researchers who work with narratives that already exist have a different task. They also must devise a narrative space that is more comprehensive than individual narratives. In her inventory, for example, Ruth lists documents on special needs, fiction or movies, and other published narratives as potential sites of inquiry for her research project. It is important to ask: What narratives produced beyond my study may inform and contextualize the narratives I compile?

A Range of Narrative Choices

David sits with yet another pile of books on narrative research studies scattered around the room. "I wish we could invite our readers into this room and just have them browse through these books for ideas and talk with us and each other about the vast array of potential narrative data sources."

"Perhaps there's a way. Let's fill this room with companions." Ruth picks up her laptop and begins to type.

✳   ✳   ✳

We left you for a lengthy stretch notebook in hand, writing potential research topics and experimenting with various narratives. "What's next?" you ask. We point toward a passage that opens into another chamber.

A few people have gathered, and one of them is brewing coffee. Others are busily working on their computers. Three people huddle around transcripts from interviews with high school adolescents whose parents do not speak English. A woman sits on the floor, watching video clips of adolescents telling stories about their early literacy experiences. Piles of DVDs spill from her tote bag. Another is watching film clips, too, but these are of teachers talking about particular literacy events in their classrooms. A woman leafs through personal narrative writing from English educators from the mid-1980s and juxtaposes those with narratives from 2009.

Talking with these researchers, you realize that any narratives of experience—memoirs, diaries, archival documents, photographs, film, transcripts, and teacher interviews elicited from curriculum documents or student work—provide data for narrative research projects. Whether eliciting, constructing, or collecting narratives, each of the researchers indicates the need for narrative data that are rich enough to provide descriptions not only of "what happens" but also of how "what happens" affects the narrator.

Beth Cross (1996) conducted life-history research with her African postgraduate colleagues through collaborative work over an extended period of time. Jalongo and Isenberg (1995) set much tighter parameters on the teacher narratives in their study. They collected autobiographical and biographical narratives of classroom teachers—stories about incidents that served as tools for reflection. Mark Freeman (1993) highlights the fact that data are limited only by the imagination of the researcher. He describes his study of nonfictional literary texts, including those written by Helen Keller, Philip Roth, and St. Augustine.

Wendy Luttrell (2003) researched, in a school designed for pregnant girls, how pregnant girls confront the representation of "the pregnant teenager." She worked with them to construct layered narratives of their evolving identities from pregnant teen to mother. The narratives consist of media collages, self-representations, journal writing, improvisational role-plays of pregnancy stories—all this compiled into a book about their individual and collective experiences.

Gubrium and Holstein (2009) developed a version of narrative ethnography to capture "everyday narrative activity that unfolds within situated interaction. It entails an acute awareness of the myriad layers of social context that condition narrative production" (p. 24). From this method, a researcher might elicit autobiographical narratives from a group of teachers to highlight their ways of storying teacher identities, constructs, beliefs, and/or actions about teaching and learning. Richert (2002) asked teachers to write, read, and reflect on narratives focused on language and cultural issues in their teaching and share these with colleagues. Leah Fowler's (2006) data were teachers' *stories of difficulty* through which they examined dilemmas in their teaching.

The *use of fiction* allows research participants to create imaginative selves as demonstrations of the potential to understand revised versions of self/selves (Lightfoot, 2004). In Lee, Rosenfeld, Mendenhall, Rivers, & Tynes's "Cultural Modeling as a Frame for Narrative Analysis" (2004), elementary schoolchildren wrote and read narratives. The children watched videos of African American storytelling and heard African American storytellers. Then, her research team selected pictures that captured cultural scripts from African American life to serve as prompts to elicit *oral stories* that they turned into written narratives.

Polkinghorne (1988) distinguishes narratives that *describe* particular phenomena from those that make causal links among narratives *to explain* phenomena. Webster and Mertova (2007) use critical event narrative analysis as a way to probe teachers' understandings of the complexities of learning and teaching. They assume narrative "is an event-driven tool of research," and, as such, "events are critical parts of people's lives, [and] using them as a main focus for research provides a valuable and insightful tool for getting at the core of what is important in that research" (p. 71).

INVESTIGATING INQUIRY SPACES: CREVICES AND EXPANSES

With experienced researchers gathered around, it seems prudent to ask for help. "I'm wondering if you have some advice in honing my study?" Stepping through the crowd, Clandinin and Connelly (1990) come toward you. "Let us talk about a way of organizing an inquiry framework to keep your study dynamic and fluid."

They ask a question: "What do narrative inquirers do?" (p. 49). Using their Deweyan view of experience, they conceptualize *situation, continuity,* and *interaction* for their inquiry framework. They explain the framework for narrative space as follows: "Our terms are *personal* and *social* (interaction); *past, present,* and *future* (continuity); combined with the notion *of place* (situation). This set of terms creates a metaphorical *three-dimensional narrative inquiry space*" (p. 50). Within this three-dimensional inquiry space, investigations can travel *inward, outward, backward, forward,* and *situated within place* (p. 49). *Inquiry space,* then, is a metaphoric way of conceptualizing a framework for an inquiry project, a space where the researcher "addresses both personal and social issues by looking inward and outward, and addresses temporal issues by looking not only to the event but to its past and to its future" (p. 50).

This conception of inquiry space is a good way to begin shaping and deepening any narrative project. Using the three-dimensional concept of inquiry can lead to explorations of contextual as well as temporal issues. Probing in this way offers extended opportunities for obtaining additional insights or information about the research topic.

Typically, a research design might be likened to a roadmap where once research questions are posed, a research process can be articulated along the road from beginning to end. In contrast, an inquiry space is multidimensional with many potential pathways in motion at the same time, one folding into others, and sometimes simultaneously. *Dimensions of understanding* in each contribute meaning to all others. In what follows, Ruth uses three dimensions—*interaction*, *continuity*, and *situation*—to see what further understandings and questions might result from her inquiry.

RUTH'S JOURNAL (SEPTEMBER 20)

INTERACTION/PERSONAL-SOCIAL

I've come to realize how competing intentions worked against our ability to communicate about Curtis's situation. We were all complicit in maintaining our individual perspectives and positions. Each of us had a felt sense that "I know better than anyone else." Rosa, Judith, Mr. Taylor, Edith, the parents—all of us entrenched ourselves in individual perspectives. Central questions remain: What prevented us from inquiring into this situation together? It would be interesting to identify the educational practices each of us privileged as we entrenched ourselves into our viewpoints. The boundaries around each viewpoint hardened rather than becoming porous! Rosa expressed her indignation that Curtis's classroom space consisted of a large refrigerator box. She wanted him out, both literally and metaphorically. Judith said: "Go ahead and try it. You'll see. *We* know better." So, Rosa coaxes Curtis out of the box and the classroom erupts into "out of control." This is *blamed* on Rosa. Mr. Taylor's priority is "safety and control first." His support of Judith and the parents certainly trumps his desire to hear from Rosa or the university.

I am implicated as the person who will provide a "second opinion" from the university, so how am I positioned? My department chair says, "We need to deal with this situation. (Rosa is the situation.) Our relationship with this school can't be compromised. We have great placements and it's a strong research site." Relationships within the classroom, within the school, between the school and university, and with the school and parents are the priority.

Much of what this incident can teach is how competing intentions work against our ability to maintain communication across differences, to interrogate practices, to listen to and support those who struggle, and to challenge institutional practices and procedures that may not be conducive to learning.

What are the multiple dimensions of past, present, and future working together? Judith says: "The university is idealistic and doesn't teach prospective teachers how to deal with tough issues that just can't be solved. . . . Who would ever imagine I would have this Curtis situation? . . . The program should forecast and problem solve some of what we will face." Judith graduated from this same program that Rosa is enrolled in, so Judith juxtaposes her teaching experiences with her university experience as she walks on these two landscapes as one. Rosa resides in "the now" of the program—to finish her student teaching experience satisfactorily—but she walks in other dimensions of her own school experiences from the past, and, as was evident in her narrative of Mr. Jameson, she also walks in some future. This is all a very complicated multitude of landscapes of time and place.

My own years of teaching bring other stories, other perspectives. I can list students and tell stories not so unlike what happened here. While there was no refrigerator box, it would be valuable to tell stories of my difficulties in dealing with some students from my 23 years of teaching high school and several in the university. What triggered my reactions to events in this situation?

Rosa's and Judith's stories foster fuller understanding of how professional and personal viewpoints shaped our individual readings of "the box." Judith describes a schoolmate when she was a child whom she believes had Down's syndrome. "There was a little room on one of the far ends of the school where several of these kids spent the day," Judith recalls. "This child would sometimes lapse into violent acts when he was frustrated." She describes the terror she felt in third grade when, on the way to school, she wouldn't give him her lunchbox. "I didn't feel like I was provoking him by saying 'no,' but he grabbed me around the throat. Just like that . . . out of the blue. . . . I'm not thinking Curtis would do that, but you never know and I was just so frightened and a bigger kid wrestled him down."

How does this tangle of Judith's and Rosa's stories explain their very different reactions to Curtis? Rosa relates her school memories of moving from school to school and her image of herself as "the quiet migrant girl." How do Rosa's experiences play here? Considering the dimension of the future—each of us has something different at stake in the tomorrows. Will Rosa stay at this school and acquiesce to Judith's viewpoint or give up her student teaching placement? Will Judith feel comfortable having Rosa take charge of the class if she does stay? What are the ramifications of Judith's work with Curtis or other students with difficulties or special needs? What action (or inaction) will I take, and how will I decide? Where do we go from here? How is the future tied up with the present moments and with each of our past experiences that inform our actions and reactions here?

SITUATION/PLACE

The classroom is spacious and sunny, with large windows framing an early morning view of the Sawtooth's jagged peaks. Student-made posters cover the walls, each poster advocating forest conservation. This is rural logging country, but the pristine forests attract locals, world-class whitewater kayakers, climbers, skiers, and fishermen. The town's economy depends on the logging camps, sawmills, and paper mills, as well as its resorts and recreational activities. The tensions are never resolved but the town thrives on its own mixed messages. Judith creates a project–based curriculum as the organizing concept of her sixth-grade English classroom. Students read about the issues from a variety of genres, including nonfiction. The titles of the units include Discovering Family and Friends, Examining Abilities and Disabilities, Finding Your Passions, and Learning About Others. Students are working through a unit titled Facing Local Issues in the Community at the time of my visit. Judith has a reputation for involving students in the questions and topics they care about and motivating them to "write out of and for life," as she describes the literacy work of her classroom.

The refrigerator box seems incongruous with the descriptions of the school, the classroom, the town. Here is a cardboard shipping box for a refrigerator, cut down to about 5' 10" with "Frigidaire" in bold, black letters on two of its four sides. The top has six skylights covered with plastic, casting beams of flores-cence to the interior. The door has a rope handle and just above it, a sign, hand painted with intricate animal faces and designs around the words "CURTIS'S SPACE—KEEP OUT!"

Spatial configurations inform social relations. This class-room space both initiates and interrupts the various interactions and how learning and teaching work in this space. The box, then, is a literal space. It is also about the constructed institutions and perspectives that theorize space as containment, boundary, bor-der crossing, and as political and ideological. Much more than physical space is at stake here. What is the relationship between physical space and social space? If I say the box is shutting out the possibility of interaction, that statement is relative to my un-derstanding of the walls as impenetrable or impermeable. Or, if Curtis perceives the walls as protective, what projections and purposes can he make about the box as his space? So, our social practices incorporate physical space but these spaces carry diver-gent meanings. The point is that space carries meaning through social practices. It's actually possible that Curtis thought of the box as a place rather than as a space. The thought of the box as a space carries enormous ideological and symbolic value. The larger place—this community of logging camps and paper mills.

AN INVITATION: REFLECTIONS ON THE INQUIRY SPACE

We hope this example demonstrates one way to create a multidi-mensional inquiry space. We encourage you to take some time to think about the dimensions of inquiry within your research project. Narrate experiences of *you*, that is, a move *inward*, on you as the researcher, and narrate how you are influenced by what is *around* you in relation to the topic you have chosen. Narrate in ways that capture how the personal and social are not binaries but are perme-able membranes—each influencing and becoming part of the other. For example, what are the grand narratives of an educational status quo and how might you confront those through petit or counter narratives? How are you implicated—what narratives have become a part of your own beliefs, values, and experiences, or how have you resisted these (which also suggests permeability)? Just as this fold between you and the social is circulating in the inquiry space, imagine that you narrate other dimensions of *interaction, continuity,* and *situation.* Narrate the puzzlements and questions that lurk in the corners. Find your silences in the recesses that are harder or impossible to articulate. Now that all these dimensions are working simultaneously and recursively, you can begin to see how this will inform or shape your narrative inquiries. Think about how narratives operate in schools and classrooms—purposes, strategies, circumstances, narrative performances and productions. How do knowledge and "authority" circulate through narratives?

"Tell Me a Story"

Experience has taught us that we don't feel completely satisfied leaving our narrative inquiries in the spaces of interpretation and reflection. While other narrative researchers may choose to write interpretive and analytic work *out of* the narratives, our choice has been to imbue the interpretation, analysis, and reflection back *into* narrative accounts. With that point made, we end this chapter with a final narrative moment from Ruth's inquiry on the boy in the box.

✳   ✳   ✳

At the moment when Rosa starts teaching, I am thinking that Judith has regularized "the box," and has segmented it somehow from her more typically political viewpoints about social learning and action as foundational in her classroom. I can't put these discrepancies into any logical relationship in my mind. Judith walks out of the classroom as Rosa walks over to Curtis's box and opens the door. He retreats and then steps forward. As he moves through the doorway, Rosa pats Curtis's shoulder. He flinches. I move to a small table at the back of the room, and before I can sit down, Curtis leaps over three desks. In the second before he turns and faces Rosa, I notice he has a pair of scissors in his hand. He points them at her. The moment is freeze framed. Rosa leans toward him, quietly, "Curtis, please let me have the scissors. You don't need them right now. Will you let me have them, please?" Curtis doesn't move. "Curtis, please. How about you go to work with your group like yesterday? You could help them again with the drawings. Your drawings are the best. Your group needs you."

The scissors move in Curtis's hand. Up, down, up again—a small glint of silver caught in the rays of fluorescence. Rosa extends her hand, palm up, a place for the scissors. The room is very still.

Curtis throws the scissors into the air and takes off, full tilt, using desks and the students in them as hurdles in his race toward the back window just behind me. As he leaps onto the windowsill, I grab the back of his shirt and slide him into my arms in a near-locked position. He squirms, then goes limp, and I sit back down with him on my lap. My arms tighten around his chest. My heart flutters at the thought that we are on the fourth floor where the old windows are thin glass that could break with no more than the heavy thud of a 50-pound boy against them. "It's okay, it's okay," I'm whispering in his ear. "I just don't want you to get hurt." The first thing I notice, beyond the heart beating in his chest and the sweet smell of peach in his hair, is Rosa staring right at me. There is a near accusation in her lifted brow. I loosen my hold on Curtis. He starts to struggle. I tighten it again. He goes quiet.

It's now I notice that the students have turned my way as if to see what I'll do. I don't have a clear plan or any insight to deal with this. "Ms. Martinez," I hear myself saying to Rosa, "Curtis and I are just fine here. Go ahead and get the groups started. We'll see if Curtis feels like drawing a little later." I hand him my pen and fumble, one-handed, for a pencil in my bag. He takes it from me. I don't remember what happens after that for the next 40 minutes of class. The smell of peach stays with me most. In my haste to give Curtis some paper, I open to a blank page in my teaching journal. Now, looking back at the three pages where he sketched during the remainder of the class, I find prehistoric-looking birds, insects I can't identify, and exotic-looking horses. Both flora and fauna are rich in detail demonstrating the artist's mind is brimming with imagination. Habitats unlike any we could point to and name on a map. Curtis draws and the groups settle into their work; Rosa moves among them asking questions and occasionally looking back at me. I don't think Curtis knows I am there any longer. He has left this world and moved into the picture world he has created in my notebook. He draws, accompanied by the drone of classroom work.

Judith reenters the classroom and walks toward me. "Curtis, come with me," she says, and walks him back toward his box. "Do you need the bathroom now? Mr. Landis will be here soon to start social studies. Do you need a little break?" Rosa turns toward me, and I see her jaw clench.

CHAPTER 5

Narrative Conversations: Questions of Efficacy

Rashid Boyd, a first-year seventh-grade teacher, laments in an English department meeting that "these kids are always out-of-control. That's what I notice in every story I've told or written about my teaching. I'm riding a wave of frenzy from minute to minute!"

Rashid shares this reflection in a teacher research seminar with his four colleagues who teach English at a middle school in the Bronx. Paul, a doctoral student, facilitates their seminar as a pilot study for his narrative research course and part of a larger narrative project that Ruth co-constructed with the English department faculty. Paul works with these teachers to understand how they experience their curricular decisions and literacy practices as enacted in the classroom. The teachers write narratives of their classroom experiences as the vehicle for their inquiry.

"I'm not certain," Rashid continues, "that telling different versions of my out-of-control phobia informs this research. Does any story count, or are we looking to tell particular stories?"

Rashid's comment leads Paul to express his concerns: "I'm struck by Rashid's question. Will any story *do*? If we control the content of stories, is that too deterministic? Is it possible to be too arbitrary? This is one of the tensions. Who controls the research agenda, questions, and the stories that get told?"

OPEN-ENDED MEANINGS: TRANSPARENCY OF ACTION

We emphasized in earlier chapters the importance of finding the foci, articulating potential questions, and naming types and sources of narratives for inquiry. We provided examples of writing, eliciting, and compiling narratives—narrative nuggets, tandem and layered tellings, sites of study, theory–story relationships, self into story, narrative elaborations, inventories, clustering narratives, and investigations of inquiry spaces.

Learning by doing is our mantra. We believe the work of narrative researchers starts and ends in the stories, questions, dilemmas, and discoveries. That said, there are some issues regarding the processes of engaging in narrative work that need further discussion. And, Rashid's question and Paul's concerns about both researchers' and participants' "control" of the research agenda give us a starting place.

AN EMERGING PRACTICE:
FACING THE UNEXPECTED ENCOUNTERS

No roadmap or methodological template constitutes an effective design for narrative inquiry. The key to the process, in fact, is shaping the instrument—the researcher—to become a traveler, a medium for questioning, stories, possibilities, and interpretations. This requires *tuning-the-self* as researcher to particular dispositions and ways of working that keep a degree of flexibility when articulating research agendas.

Maintain Degrees of Flexibility Within an Articulation of Purpose

Paul asks, "I'm not sure the research is moving in the direction I proposed in this pilot." We emphasize how important it is to resist a preliminary design so rigid that the paths of the research journey cannot diverge when the unexpected tempts the researcher and participants to take a different direction than originally imagined. We remind Paul that his original proposal was a narrative that *projected* possible ways of imagining direction for the research. "It is a *proposal* after all," David tells him.

We typically ask for a 3 to 5 page overview describing purposes for the narrative inquiry, suggesting big ideas that might be explored, forecasting a range of participants and types of narrative that might provide insightful "data," and naming some potential structures (interviews, study groups, focus groups, archived compilations) for eliciting the data. The proposal in this conception is an *investigative walk* that *narrates* an imagined research landscape. The proposal is not a contract. We remind Paul: Play out the journey in your mind first. What do you want to learn, whom do you want to learn with, whose narratives will help you learn, and why does it matter? Only later will research questions make sense (and these will change throughout the research process) as will a *continuing conversation* with relevant literature for review.

In his proposal, Paul wrote, "I hope to compose a tapestry of English teachers' stories about how they enact their beliefs about literacy curriculum and instructional practices. Working in a Bronx middle school, how do these four very unique and different actor-teachers perform their lived experiences through their teaching narratives?"

"Where in this investigative-walk-as-proposal do you contract with us to make certain that teachers focus their narratives on curriculum or instructional practices exclusively?" Ruth smiles at Paul, waiting for a reply.

"Let's look at one of the narratives Rashid wrote," Paul leafs through the transcripts, "and see what you think."

Rashid's Narrative: There's More to the Story (November 20)

> "Okay guys, for the third time, get your writer's notebooks on your desks. Now, please!" In what seems like a long time, maybe two-thirds of the kids have notebooks out. I wait, cross-legged on the back of a student desk. Lenny shouts out: "Love that red shirt, dude!"
>
> "I'll wear it every day if you'll just take out your notebook like I ask. So, we ready?"
>
> I pull out my notebook: "Let me read this paragraph I wrote yesterday, and you can give me some advice." I read: "Marsha told me a secret the other night. I wasn't supposed to tell anyone but here I am standing in front of William who will really want to know that Marsha likes him. And, William isn't my best friend but this could be a tipping point in our relationship."
>
> With my teacher double-vision, I look out while I'm reading to students who rifle through bags, heads down on the desk.

Lenia is lipglossing, and Ray's fingers are nested in Marina's hair. I continue reading. "I was ready to put the moves on Marsha and hook up with her and now this." Students glance around the room. Some snickers and grins.

"So I don't know where to take this. Should I tell what comes next or build suspense? Should I do a flashback that shows a moment in my relationship with either William or Marsha? Help me here. I need your help!" At this point I look right at the kids. No response.

"So, start giving me suggestions."

Nothing. A few more kids put their heads down. Felicia and Tiffany are whispering and passing lipstick or eyeliner.

"Anyway," I continue, "I could use some advice. Renaldo, help me here."

"I dunno. Maybe get rid of William? Kill him off!"

"No!" says Alicia. "You should fight for the girl."

I ask Fredericka, who has her head down. She looks up and shrugs.

"Well, I got a little advice, but it shouldn't be this hard! I'm going to ask you to get some advice on what you wrote yesterday. Get into your writing groups. Listen to what your friends have to say and then work from their advice."

There is a blur for me now. Students make their way into groups but I spend the rest of my time picking up hairbrushes and cellphones, begging students to stop talking and start working on this, tapping shoulders to get heads off the desk, and breaking up an argument between Flora and Marc. I try to refocus the class when I know it isn't working and put these questions on the board:

1. What's working?
2. What do you want to improve?
3. Specific suggestions?

This doesn't help much. I'm happy for the bell. "Wait!" Rosalinda shouts, "What ever happened with Marsha and William?"

Students rush out the door, but there is just this little moment of joy left hanging in my chest!

Reading for Stories Nested Within Stories

The reason Paul facilitated the teacher research group at Rashid's school was to learn more about the potential of narrative inquiry to serve as a professional education resource for teachers as they explored their practices in literacy education. And, while Rashid's narrative describes his concerns with students' lack of focus, he does give us more than a glimpse into his instructional practices. Here's some of what we know: Students keep writing in notebooks and share their work in peer response groups. Rashid teaches students to give feedback to one another, and he attempts to model how to give useful feedback. His attention is directed primarily at student action and reaction, but that does not mean that literacy practices are absent.

Rashid's story brings us into the classroom, and we see him in action with the students. Not everything may go the way he hopes, but we are able to *come to, attune ourselves to the moments he shares* with us. His story matters. The fact that he questions its value provides insight into how he experiences the classroom in this first year of his teaching.

Researchers and tellers of stories invent and reinvent the research journey by continuously reading, rereading, and asking questions that keep the inquiry open. The research agenda is invented in the *doing* and in the reinvestigation and re-seeing. For Paul, this experience of looking for narratives nested in narratives led him to reflect: "If researchers and narrators maintain the flexibility to look for the stories within stories, the richness seems to emerge." Looking for or creating stories within stories is part of the interpretive work in narrative inquiry.

Positioning the Researcher's "I" in the Inquiry Process

Possibly no place more than in narrative research is it important for the researcher to acknowledge the "I." Bringing back the "I," the long-lost subject of both researchers and the tellers of stories, adds an essential dimension in narrative inquiry.

Paul says, "The curves and turns of decision making and impressions are definitely part of the research story for me. The research and the researcher feel like they are intertwined, like dancer and dance."

Our general words of advice: Invite your readers into the worlds of your research planning and process. Show your participants as part of the research story and describe your processes of negotiation. Share issues related to the difficulties encountered when gathering and receiving narratives, and, as necessary, show your willingness to change course in response to participants. Let your readers know who the eye/the "I" is who has conceived, compiled, selected, and written into the very fabric of the research project.

Researchers are influenced by a variety of thoughts and feelings that result from values, deeply held beliefs, social histories, and experiences in both producing and receiving stories. To put forward the layers of making decisions pointing and gesturing at selected phenomena—all this is part of the story that may be told.

Reflexivity. To engage in reflexive examination is to commit to including your "selves" in the process of knowledge creation. Reflexivity is an act of deep reflection on the values, beliefs, persons, and certainly the ideologies that influence the way a researcher engages in the research. We say to Paul: "Keep reminding the reader of the presence of the 'I'/eye guiding and nudging this inquiry along throughout the process."

Paul laughs. "A bit like the Wizard of Oz behind the curtain." Beliefs and assumptions generated by experiential, societal, and formal theories shape and inform how we read the texts of our research, and our readers will be interested.

"In the actual report," asks Paul, "do I position myself within and alongside their narratives to make my values and beliefs known? I'm not sure I know how to write the 'I' into my study except the obvious ways that seem a bit like token gestures to me."

"Well, reflexivity reveals the interactions between you, your participants, and the topics of inquiry and the data. One way to accomplish this is by writing multilayered texts. There are guides to help you," David gestures to the bookcases behind him. "Turn to other writers to trigger your own ways of imagining how to do this."

Metanarrative and Commentary. Reflexivity in research writing requires the researcher to present the multidirectional nature of the process. Most often, reflexivity is enacted through the research writer's instigating an examination of self or the research process, recognizing the biases, forces of socialization, assumptions, or any number of influences that make visible his/her place in shaping and controlling the work. Reflexivity may be woven through or alternate with the narratives, interpretive work, explanations of methodology, or review of literature. The key is to learn about the available resources for crafting reflexivity into the research writing. Frankly, we find more engaging help from metafiction than from most research reports we've read.

In *Cat's Cradle*, when Vonnegut (1998) stops to describe facetiously the "shape" of the plot within his novel by drawing elaborate lines and curlicues, he is working in a reflexive tradition extending at least as far back as the mid-18th-century novel *Tristram Shandy* (Sterne, 2009/1759), in which the narrator makes it humorously clear he is aware of the kind of narrative moves he is struggling to make.

A multitude of contemporary metafictional novels foreground the process of creating them—Kundera's *Book of Laughter and Forgetting* (1988), Calvino's *If on a Winter's Night a Traveler* (1970), Borges's *Ficciones* (1969), and our perennial favorite, T. O'Brien's *The Things They Carried* (1990). These novels are labeled metafiction (Currie, 1995) primarily because they explicitly theorize the nature of narrative in the process of telling a tale.

O'Brien's *The Things They Carried* provides many examples of metanarrative as the sense-making function of story is interwoven in the context of O'Brien's experience in the Vietnam War. The book examines problems of observation and memory, and the relationship between what he calls "story truth" and "happening truth."

O'Brien's reflexivity focuses on the nature of story throughout and between his stories. Story, for him, is not only a form of analysis and reflection, but also an art form for making sense of experiences that almost can seem too powerful to be captured in language. The interwoven metanarrative and the narration of Vietnam experiences work together to portray how *what is* can be hard to separate from *what seems*. O'Brien's narrator in the short story "Good Form" describes it this way:

> It's time to be blunt. I'm forty-three years old, true, and I'm a writer now, and a long time ago I walked through the Quang Ngai Province as a

foot soldier. Almost everything else is invented. But it's not a game, it's a form . . . I want you to feel what I felt. I want you to know why story-truth is truer sometimes than happening-truth. . . . What stories can do, I guess, is make something present. (pp. 179–180)

It is, in O'Brien's words, "story-truth" (cf. Berger & Luckmann, 1967) that is examined through the metanarrative.

Paul reads an example of his exploration on reflexivity. "It's just an attempt at self-awareness, but I can start to imagine how I might weave it into the telling or put it alongside the stories that Rashid tells."

Paul's Journal Entry: (Re)Membering and Reflexivity (December 9)

Rashid asked me a startling question today. "I start to wonder if I have the strength to stick with teaching. Do I have enough passion and commitment? I don't want to say it, but I think good teachers have this magical quality. I'm not sure it can be learned." I recognized that this question was deep inside of me, too, in a double-visioned way. I'd felt the same sentiment as I watched Rashid struggle with his teaching. The overwhelming sensation of dread, of that feeling right before breaking out into a cold sweat. Where was the physical sensation coming from?

I had a moment when I heard, almost in cacophony with his, my own voice admitting, in very similar words, the same feeling to my father during my first year of teaching. Rashid's question/my question/the eternal question of whether we are good enough, committed enough, strong enough—it all came rushing in, deep into my bones. In watching and hearing Rashid, I see myself. Suddenly, when I see Jamal in Rashid's class acting with the "who needs you, anyway" attitude, I think of my student Oscar. Rashid calls, "Hey, you guys, remember me? I'm here." I hear my own voice in the first year of teaching, calling out and feeling out of control. I feel his feelings. Rashid's and my experiences blend together. Do we learn about ourselves through others' stories or by how our stories are called up through someone else's narrative?

Paul teaches us that recording all that he can conjecture about his psychological, social, and personal experiences—the narratives through which he (re)searches his "I"—provides rehearsals toward reflexivity.

INTERPRETIVE TURNS: PROVOKING A HOLISTIC

A way to understand any narrative, as we have said earlier, is to look around, behind, above, under, to the side of, and to the other potential stories that are nested inside any one story—only then do we have a full encounter with the story. We also demonstrated some dimensions of narrative in Chapter 1 that have salience for interpretation. "But," Paul asks, "how do I approach the interpretation?"

"You've already explored the narratives in multiple ways— finding Rashid's stories within stories, placing your stories at the side of his stories, and exploring Rashid's larger story behind his out-of-control story. All these are part of the interpretive turns you are already taking," David points out.

Interpretation is going on constantly and recursively in narrative inquiry. Interpretation is the habit of critical reflection. It isn't a linear process—collect narratives as data and then perform some textual analysis on them and articulate findings or conclusions. There are many possible frameworks for interpretation and analysis that others have written about and that serve as references for designing interpretive plans (Daiute & Lightfoot, 2004; Lieblich, Tuval-Mashiach, & Zilber, 1998; Ochs & Capps, 2001; Webster & Mertova, 2007). The interpretive variety and creative demands in determining ways to work with raw data can be a bit overwhelming. Paul asks: "Where do I start?" The answer is: "You already have."

"What next?" Paul asks.

"Let's take a look at a narrative I wrote after visiting one of Rashid's classes. After reading, let's determine what we are able to notice. What reveals meaning for you? How do you describe your encounter with this narrative? "

RUTH'S NARRATIVE OF RASHID'S CLASS (NOVEMBER 17)

Today, Mr. Boyd begins class with a question: "Do you think Willie Bodega's dream is realistic?" Students are reading *Bodega*

Dreams by Ernesto Quinonez (2000). Mr. Boyd tried to establish literature circles early in the school year but thought that he might have better luck "keeping all the students focused on one thing that is of high interest to them. I'm just not skilled enough yet to have all those balls in the air at once. It's hard to plan and to keep the kids in line and doing what they've been asked to do. I'll work gradually toward that."

Mr. Boyd asks again. "Help me here. All eyes on my pencil. I'll ask once more. Are Willie Bodega's dreams realistic?"

If we hold this scene still a moment, here's what you will notice: All eyes are on Mr. Boyd but no one is answering his question. It is noon. Post-lunch lethargy fogs the room. There is a knock at the door. "Excuse me, Mr. Boyd. Can I see Stephanie?" The students are chatting again.

Mr. Boyd restates the question again after Stephanie leaves. "Again, are Willie Bodega's dreams realistic? We aren't going anywhere, so answer up."

Finally, Jillian blurts out, "He stepped out of his family tradition and made money. If it's drug money, does it matter? That doesn't change the dream. He's the Robin Hood and has a good purpose."

From two separate parts of the room we hear groans and comments: "That don't make it right!" "He's fixing up Harlem. We need him in the Bronx!" Laughter. "We take some of that, too," Miguel blurts out. "Bodega gets rid of that loser Fischman whose takin' all the loot." "Yeah, but de woman gets in the way. Vera, Vera and there goes Bodega forgettin'." "His head in his pants." They are on a roll. Gesturing. Laughing. Pointing at crotches. Lucille stands up and wiggles her bum.

"Okay, enough," says Mr. Boyd. "Let's cool this down. You're getting out of the story and my question."

"Mister, mister. Uh, Sir. He fall on his little love knees to Vera and loses everything." Hands shoot up and the side banter starts. Comments come from everywhere and sexual energy fills the room. Some think Bodega loses the dream for the girl; others think he was really just a druggie; still others see him as the Robin Hood.

"Shhh . . . shhh . . . shhh. No side conversations. Knees forward and facing me. My question: Was the dream realistic? You aren't answering that. Slow it down. Take a breath. Miguel, eyes here. Stop talking to each other now. Let's settle in. Let's take a few minutes, and you can write down your response to the question."

Terence is agitated. "I had something else to say. Why can't we say more?"

"Put it in the parking lot," Mr. Boyd tells him. "Write about it. Okay, next 10 minutes. Just write. No talking. I mean it. Settle down."

As I write about this moment, I remember something else: The question doesn't lead to any particular understanding or resolution by the end of class. Students have lost interest in Bodega's story and dream. They've written, shared out in some haphazard manner. Now, their notebooks and pencils are packed up. Some fidget; others flash hand signals to each other; Simon reads a book; Paul plays a computer game, hiding his hand-held device under his desk. Mr. Boyd surveys the room. "Good job, today. Good work. Finish Bodega tonight and we'll continue discussion tomorrow. Okay, don't forget." Tap. Tap. Tap. His finger points to the assignment on the board. Everyone is waiting for the bell.

Features Worth Pondering

The ways of paying attention to (encountering or interpreting) this narrative are infinite. But, *the ways of paying attention determine what you are able to see.* We offer a demonstration by choosing three concepts and using them, briefly, as interpretive lenses to see what features each brings into view.

> *Salience.* Begin exploring the narrative by listing moments that resonate. What stays with you? What images, bits of dialogue, moments in the narrative linger and endure? Paul points out several salient moments that would lead to further interpretive turns: (1) "Tap. Tap. Tap. . . . Everyone is waiting for the bell; (2) "Let's take a few minutes and you can write down your response to the question"; (3) "I had something else to say. Why can't we say more?" "Put it in

the parking lot," Mr. Boyd tells him; (4) Ruth stepping out
of the direct narration to say: "As I write about this moment, I remember something else: The question doesn't
lead to any particular understanding or resolution by the
end of class. Students have lost interest in Bodega's story
and dream." Stay with what is salient and write about it—
the striking, the noticeable, and the relevant.

Incompleteness. What does the narrator gloss over? What seems
implicit but not stated? Are there obvious silences? What
puzzlements linger and what more do you want to know?
How does the narrative reveal the narrator?

Emphasis. What events, dialogue, memories are intensified
through repetition, vivid imagery, dialogue? Is there a center (focal point) to be exhumed from underneath the details
of this narrative moment? What reveals meaning?

These are just a few examples of interpretive turns that might
help a researcher follow leads and hunches, and produce other narratives and interpretations. Interpretation of narratives is not about
"getting it right"; each of the examples shows different investigatory
interests and opportunities.

MULTIPLE TELLINGS ENRICH THE INTERPRETIVE TURN

Another interpretive path can be taken by providing side-by-side
narratives of the same events. We use the tandem or side-by-side tellings as a form of interpretation. In what follows, Rashid narrates in
the third person in an attempt to stand back and see himself in the
classroom.

RASHID'S NARRATIVE (NOVEMBER 17)

Rashid is living his out-of-control dream again!!! He begins
by asking students what seems like a simple question: Is Willie
Bodega's dream realistic? Rashid has decided that whole-class
instruction may be best for now. He realizes that even with the
whole-group novel, attention is fractured. He plays the words

fractured and *fragmented* off his tongue. The question about Willie hangs in the room. Rashid has the students' eyes on him. He uses the "eyes on my pencil" and "eyes on me" and the "knees forward" that he learned from a veteran teacher. But, what he wasn't taught or didn't learn was how to get these young students' minds focused.

"What about Willie?" he asks again. Jillian answers. She thinks Willie is a Robin Hood and that sets all the students chattering. And with one student shouting out over others, the whole conversation suddenly turns from who Willie is to what he does for Vera, and then the sexual connotations start. Rashid is working hard to gain control. "Okay. Help me here. Cool down." He knows they have left the question behind. Rashid wonders how to get back on track. What's a way to get their energy? By now the students are in side conversations. Even though most are talking about the book, they seem out of control. How can Rashid harness this energy and keep the conversation going? He starts thinking: What if I move them quickly into groups and create a character map of Willie? What if I ask them to write a letter from Willie to Vera? Would that just stay sexual since they are thinking that way now? What if I ask them to divide into groups and write a character sketch on Willie?

Rashid is just not sure where to move next, and the students are getting further away from the question. Rashid has ideas swirling in his mind for what to do next, but nothing seems right. He takes the easy way out and the students know it. "Write about what you are thinking," he says. The students settle but their ideas wilt away as well. Rashid has lost them, but he is relieved that the wave of energy has receded.

The most common interpretive turn would be to compare the narratives. We suggest the side-by-side narratives *are an interpretation*. The researcher's task is to bring readers into a well-constructed interpretive space where Ruth and Rashid work out what they have learned from the shared experience. In this version the researcher narrates the entire experience rather than interprets the research experience.

Working Toward a Suppleness of Theory: Little by Little

"Another issue," Paul says to Ruth and David, "is that I'm not certain how to work with theory nor do I think I know a theory or theorist well enough to actually be able to use theory effectively. Other than reading deeply, are there other ways to work with theory as I continue to learn?"

"Theories and theorists may serve as *lenses for inquiry*," David suggests. "Examining narratives through multiple lenses encourages a researcher not only to deconstruct but also to reconstruct alternative explanations of individual narratives. The process provides principles and interpretive practices that allow for more complex notions of agency, for example, or any other explorations you are taking up in narrative."

Ruth continues, "We could list dozens of studies where various lenses become a way of reinvesting in and re-seeing the data of research projects. It strikes me that theory is positioned in research reports as curator of high or right-minded ideas rather than as *provocateur*. Too often it feels like Theory, personified, stands above or off to the side wagging a finger, reminding a researcher not to go too far off the path of Theory's wisdom. Theory should be used with suppleness."

"I'm thinking that I want to read more deeply into Bourdieu because of his theorizing of social practices and particularly the arbitrariness of pedagogic action and the theorizing about ways of keeping order. I think it will be helpful to start by narrating stories of how theory can provide a lens to see common things anew," Paul suggests.

"Let's look at an example that might help you, Paul," Ruth says as she pulls open a file drawer.

A Trail of Evidence

Here's an excerpt from Roberta Lenger Kang's experimentation in working through Bourdieu's difficult concepts of *structuring structures*, *objective structures,* and *habitus.* Notice how Roberta narrates her understanding of these concepts by re-reading the literal sign, "Please Keep off Grass."

NARRATING BOURDIEU (ROBERTA LENGER KANG)

There is an open area of grass outside my apartment building that has a sign placed in the center that states: Please Keep off Grass. While this sign may appear to be an objective message, this simple statement embodies the values and desires of a particular cultural group—namely, the co-op board—and was placed on the grassy area to send a very specific message: This sign, or structure, privileges the existence of and regulates the interaction with open spaces. This sign communicates that open spaces are to be enjoyed through viewing, and the longer the sign stands, the more we accept and eventually embrace this message. However, this sign also communicates that the members of the community cannot be trusted to maintain a safe environment without "proper" supervision. To those who initiated the placement of the sign, it represents preservation. To those who are subjected to the sign, it suggests suppression. To everyone, this sign contains a symbolic power over the community that restricts the movement of individuals under implicit threat of prosecution by those governing.

Of course, I never think about this when I pass by the sign. I just keep thinking how pretty the grass looks. *Structuring structures* are statements or language acts that reproduce the perspectives of those who create them for those who encounter them. The fact that I rarely engage intellectually with the directive to keep off the grass is an example of how my own thinking has been structured by the sign, and the millions like it all around me. "Please Keep off Grass" is an example of a most fundamental concept that Bourdieu asserts: that of structuring structures. Our basic understanding of the confidence we have in language, is that words have agreed-upon meanings and represent unseen systems that reflect, create, and reproduce power. *Objective structures,* or uses of language that appear to be free of bias, not only are full of the biases that exist within the denotations and connotations of the words that make them, but generate and reproduce specific perspectives.

Observed structures, language practices, and literacy events should be seen as generative and active agents instead of stagnant, negligible objects because our actions and interactions impact our perceptions, which impact our actions, again and again. We must remember that there is no such thing as an objective, unbiased, or impartial interaction. All actions and interactions are filtered through the perception and experiences of individuals, and all actions and interactions are created when external activities are internalized. For Bourdieu, behaviors don't just exist in an objective space. They are the products of the beliefs, feelings, values, and experiences of the individual (and by extension—the community, and the society). People are social beings who live in varying degrees of community—in families, in the workforce, in schools, in shared public and private spaces. They are individuals who negotiate the world with other people.

In order to negotiate the world with other people, we have and are governed by structured, growing, and connected knowledge that comes to life the more we interact with one another. This, Bourdieu calls *habitus*. Habitus guarantees the correctness and durability of practices over time. Therefore, when we closely examine the behavior and the language structure that people use, it is possible to identify the thinking that led them to make certain decisions. Habitus ensures that a person's past experiences are always with him or her in his or her present moment. Those past experiences, always accumulating, create a system of perceptions, thoughts, and actions that tend to regulate a person's appropriate behavior over time. We behave the way we do more because of our internal system than because of external rules or norms. Because of this internal system, we create all of the thoughts, feelings, and perspectives that influence our actions without having to fully weigh the details of every single decision. And, we keep off the grass.

Before any of us can know theory as a *supple presence* in our research and in our lives, we must live with it, articulate it through "objects" and experiences, and story it as a way of understanding how it works in the world.

Persistent (Re)Searching:
The Circular Paths in Narrative Inquiry

We are constantly reminded during any narrative inquiry project that we are traveling on obscured paths toward somewhere that cannot be fully named at the beginning of our research journeys. At any given moment, it may feel as though we have constructed a narrative, an interpretation, or a method for collection and analyses. Suddenly, the path of "constructed" feels finalized and we turn our gaze to another part of the landscape that has more to teach us. *The doing* of research is *recursive work*, in which we constantly are learning through the narratives and the methods what paths to take next or how to double back to a path taken before to see again what wasn't seen on previous excursions.

CHAPTER 6

Storying Us

RANDI DICKSON

In this chapter, Randi narrates her journey into the places and spaces she inhabits with her research participants. We appreciate her attention to details. Stories of Mona—"the hundreds of birds that Mona feeds." Mona hunched over a magazine, forgetting to eat. Sue, like Mona, with "nature moved indoors" where feathers and stones are captured by Randi's narrative eye. Stories reside in a snowy night, a dark desert, and in cups of steaming coffee. Randi's attention to the whisper of stories around Mona and Sue launches the contexts of their lives in ways that more fully help us understand the lived experiences they bring to teaching and how their lives are enriched because of their teaching and passion for learning.

I tell two stories that invoke the process and tensions often present in gathering data. Embedded in each of these stories are other stories that I hope will illuminate something of the nature of my participants, Mona and Sue; the nature of our relationship; and the nature of the research itself. Making space for these stories is a way to explore my own subjectivity and make sense of my process of constructing knowledge about these women for myself and my readers. In these stories we get a glimpse into the worlds of Mona and Sue, but we also begin to see the impact the work is having on the researcher herself—which helps shed light on the text I eventually will fashion.

MONA (DECEMBER 16–18, 1997)

Things are covered with dust, piles and stacks abound, nature of all varieties has moved indoors and hangs on walls, is gathered in baskets, is piled on the floor. It is random and messy, connected by cobwebs and layered with film—one might think this last is because she is old (81) but that is not so. It was always this way. "There are so many more important things to do than keep house," she once told me when I was helping her clean up for her annual move home to Tucson, Arizona, following another spring semester of teaching at Southampton College, New York. It is a lesson she could teach me. How could she find time to read the piles of myriad magazines stacked next to every chair if she were worrying about straightening and cleaning? And there are many chairs—I count eight from the one I sit in now next to the window watching the hundreds of birds Mona feeds. They fly up suddenly and I see Mona's black cat stroll by and watch them settle in again on the feeders that hang from trees and stand on posts. When I arrived here in Bon Carbo, a tiny town in southern Colorado, we walked into the living room to sit. "Which chair is yours?" I asked, not wanting to take her accustomed seat. "None of them," she said. "I sit in them all."

Last night driving up here the world seemed so different. It was late and I had left my home and family some 1,600 miles and 14 hours earlier. Turning off the main road onto a dirt one covered with frozen slush and snow, I was plunged into sudden darkness. I was tired and not just a little frightened. In the small rental car that I had gotten at the Denver airport nearly 5 hours before, I was hoping I did not get stuck or slide off into the ravine that hugged the right side of the road. I played a cassette from an interview with Mona when she came to visit in May and I hoped that her voice would both soothe me and bring me to her. My directions were sketchy and there was no one for miles—nowhere to phone and only occasionally a flicker of light high in the mountains to the left side. I drove on wondering if I'd gone too far. The sky was lit with a just waning moon and it made the stretches of snow shine eerily. I was wondering why anyone would choose to live in such isolation, especially someone alone and old.

But this morning it is different. It is no longer threatening and dark and isolated, but sunny and clear with striking vistas of snow-covered mountains, the Sangre de Cristo. I take my coffee outside and breathe deeply of the cold, still air. It is incredibly peaceful. The lack of any humans nearby allows the birds to settle around in swarms. It is a place she has come to rest from a world of people who always wanted her so, who would have sucked her dry if she'd let them. People always flocked to Mona, needing to be around her, to call her friend, to boast of knowing her. She has escaped it all now. She lives among her birds, her dog, her cat, her books, and her magazines. She is resting from that other world, but the mind is as active as ever.

Next to her chairs I pick up current issues of *National Geographic, The New Yorker, Science News, Time, The Nation, Nature Conservancy, Arizona Highways, Parabola, Discover, Smithsonian, National History Magazine*—the list goes on. I flip through them and more often than not I see her familiar handwriting making notes in the margins. Arrows, dots, underlinings mark the pages and inside the front cover or on it, a brief cataloging of the issue to remind herself—a quote, a list of things to remember.

And everywhere there are the books. Everywhere. Spilling from every shelf, lines of them marching across the floor. The titles are often of science and nature and cultures—of teaching and learning mixed in with fiction and children's books. I pull four off the shelf in a closet (a walk-in lined with shelves of texts—like stacks in a library). The first one I open is *The Language Experience Approach to the Teaching of Reading*, and inside, on the top of the title page, she has written *my* name with the word "birthday" and "Nov. 8" with a circle around it. It is a book she used 20 years ago when I first knew her and used to sit in on her education classes at Southampton College. I nod to myself that my name should pop out from this first book I open. In the mystical, magical world of Mona, a self-proclaimed "witch" who always marked her driveways with broom sticks, this does not surprise. Her driveway here, marked with a bright yellow "witch crossing" sign (a witch riding a broomstick), helped bring me to her last night.

Under the circle with my name she has written, "See that each child succeeds"; "Find your words in books and magazines";

"Help each other"; "move around and share"—all tenets of the language experience approach she pioneered. I open to a scrap of paper. In bright pink marker she has underlined sentences that inform and reflect her philosophy: "The teacher must avoid being the authority. Her teaching must be such that the group is never intimidated by the tyranny of a right *teacher* answer—one that the group dare not question; her role is agitator. . . . In this capacity, she asks and asks again: 'What do you think? Why do you think so?'"

I step out of the closet to refill my coffee cup. Mona is sitting in a chair by the kitchen table hunched over a magazine, marker pen in hand, putting dots next to an article in this week's *New Yorker*.

"How about some breakfast, Mona Joy?" I say.

"Oh, yes!" she answers. "I forgot that we're supposed to eat."

*   *   *

This second morning, December 17, I am still in bed. It is early—early enough to see the sunrise light up the tops of the mountains a soft rose—early enough for the nearly full moon to still be out in the sky above the far off peaks.

I pour a cup of coffee and return to my bed to read, but Mona has seen me stir and shortly after she pushes my door open carrying a big pile. She drops armfuls of stuff on my bed. She has been busy even before sunrise.

She has found some of the things I have been asking about: the *Look* magazine dated April 19, 1966 (35 cents) in which there are the pictures of her and her four children with President Johnson when she received the National Teacher of the Year Award. She says, "I told them that all of my children *had* to come with me" ("and I made them pay for it, too," she adds) because "they had all taught me and helped me be the teacher I was."

She brings in stacks of large 8 x 10 black and white photos taken in her classroom and in Washington, all from the year when she won the award for her teaching of first graders at the Flowing Wells School in Arizona. Included in the stack are the laminated letters each child wrote to President Johnson, letters Mona later was told circulated the White House for many months. We begin reading them, laughing at their directness. "What a kick," she says. "Listen to this: "Write all day/Until your head aches/ Thinking like a President/love Michele."" I read from one I've picked up: "Dear President Johnson, I like to know if all the war is past. Is it? Love Teri Lynn Throp."

We are lost for a while in these letters and pictures and the stories that go with them. Now it is afternoon and we have just come up for air, nudged again by my reminder that "we've forgotten to eat." We have spent the morning hours poring through her boxes, wiping off cobwebs, dusting off covers, gently unfolding crinkled yellow pages—a life in scribbled notes, annotated articles, children's and teachers' work. She digs out copy after copy of *Poets and Writers* magazine and *Teachers and Writers Collaborative*. She has continued to subscribe to both long since she has left her classrooms. As she tells me, "I like to support them."

"Here, take these. Nobody wants them. I'm glad to have them used."

Each new thing she finds launches her into another place and time. My pulse is racing slightly when we come across a whole scrapbook of articles from the year surrounding her award. It feels a little like opening King Tut's tomb or the discovery of cave paintings. How will I sift through it all in the short time I have here? How can I carry back these artifacts of the teaching life, so indicative of the life itself? Is it okay to take things that her own children and grandchildren will someday perhaps want? Will they someday want to sift through these papers rediscovering who this woman was—their mother, their grandmother, other people's friend, and *always* teacher? I cannot say—but begin to make piles all over my bed and to think about a big box to ship them home in.

✳   ✳   ✳

December 18th. I am lost in some time warp, living in Mona's past and surfacing occasionally to enjoy her present. This morning I have walked around her rooms to catalog what hangs, sits, perches from almost every space. Here is some of what I see: *feathers* (hundreds!); *owls*: stuffed, statues, eyes looking at me everywhere; *puppets*; *masks* from many cultures; *a pelican skin* (a mark of honor given to her); *skulls*, bones, skeletons; *baskets*: hanging, sitting, full of shells, stones, rocks, pebbles; *wall hangings* of beads, cloth; *crystals* of all shapes and sizes catching light and reflecting rainbows; *children's artwork*; *ads* torn from magazines and newspapers for travel to exotic places (Inca caves) taped randomly all over bathrooms, kitchen, bedroom walls; *brooms* (she has a vast collection); *elephant stools* (from her year in Botswana, Africa, with her son, a doctor, and his family); *musical instruments* of every kind, many made by students and a nephew, or collected on travels through Africa, Mexico, the American Southwest; a *bear skin and head* thrown over a pool table ("it came with the house," she says of the table); a huge elephant *femur* she *"HAD"* to bring back from Africa.

Framed: Certificate from Lyndon B. Johnson appointing her "Member of the Commission on Presidential Scholars," April 5, 1966, and signed by the President; Certificate from the "Office of the Mayor, City of Tucson," Congratulations on Being Teacher of the Year May 5, 1966; Plaque: Expression of Appreciation for Many Contributions to Southampton College Class of '72.

Pictures, Pictures, Pictures: of friends, of places, but mostly of family—a husband, 4 children, spouses and ex-spouses, 11 grandchildren.

※   ※   ※

This morning, my last one here, Mona and I sit in chairs by a sunny window. Crystals catch the light and cover us with rainbows.

We have been sipping our coffee and talking. She has been telling me of a recent conversation she had with her soul, "sitting right here in this chair." "I was asking my soul," she said, "if I'd done what I came here to do, learned what I needed to."

"And what is that, Mona?" I ask.

"I guess to do what my father always said: 'To find the God hiding in everyone.' To learn not to make judgments about people. Refrain from making judgments. I think those judgments can really wipe people out."

We sit quietly for a minute, taking this in. The sun sifts softly through the window, warming us both.

SUE (DECEMBER 28, 1997)

It is snowing and I watch the huge flakes build inches on the porch rail the light illuminates. "Wouldn't it be nice to be snowed in," Sue says, as she climbs the stairs to bed. "Why not?" I think, surrounded by my own books as well as one of Sue's I picked up off the counter: Belenky, Clinchy, Goldberger, and Tarule's *Women's Ways of Knowing* (1996). I know I could easily stay busy here for days.

She disappears to bed upstairs and I continue watching the snow, taken back to the last time I lay in this bed, watching the snow fall then too. It was March 15, 1997. I had taken a train from East Hampton to New York City and from there a Greyhound bus to New Paltz in upstate New York. It was a cold gray day and the forecast was for substantial snow. My plan was to spend the night at Sue's, who was then 82 and living alone on 10 acres of property at the top of a very long driveway. I was going to drive us in her car the next day down to Sag Harbor where I would begin my oral history interviews with her.

When I arrived at the single-room Trailways bus station in New Paltz in early evening, I was tired from traveling over 6 hours and was ready for a glass of wine and some food. I hoped Sue would be waiting at the bus stop, but when she was nowhere in sight, I went in and phoned (she lived about 25 minutes away over the mountain). My heart sank a little when she answered. She sounded anxious and in a hurry. "You just caught me," she said. "I was about to leave for Chaffe's [her son, who lives about an hour south]. There's going to be a lot of snow and I don't want to be snowed in."

"But Sue," I protested, "I'm at the bus station in New Paltz."

"There'll be another bus back to New York," she said. "Just turn around and go back or you can come with me to Chaffe's."

I took a deep breath, ready to start sniffling. "I can't, Sue. I've been traveling most of the day and I'm tired and hungry and I'm not going anywhere else tonight. You can go, of course, but I'd like to stay here. Is there any way for me to get to your house?"

"Al," she said. "I'll call him and he can come get you."

A half hour later, a pleasant-looking man with a thick mustache, eyes with sparkle, and a hoarse voice, walked into the empty waiting room and asked, "Randi?" "Sure am," I said, so grateful to be rescued. Another half hour later, the three of us were sitting around Sue's kitchen table pouring brandy into glasses and discussing the forecast. Relaxed from being in each other's company and from the warming glow of the brandy, we decide to take our chances with the snow and stay put.

Sometime in the early predawn hours I woke up and looked out the upstairs window. Snow was falling and all I could see was white. When I awoke again, I could smell Sue's strong coffee brewing. Glancing out the same window on the way to the bathroom I saw huge shadowy forms, 3 or 4 feet tall, crossing from the woods over the driveway, their tracks webbed and big in the snow. "Sue, Sue, look out the window!" I called. "Wild turkeys," she said, and we both gazed in wonder.

When I awake on this December morning though, the snow is beautiful, but hardly enough to trap us in. I wander around the house in much the same way I meandered through my days at Mona's, sitting on the floor next to bookcases and shelves and stacks and cabinets and randomly looking, reading, recording . . .

In many ways Sue's homes (she had one in Montauk at the easternmost tip of Long Island for many years and I often went there for overnight stays) are similar to Mona's. In Montauk, much of the decor was also "nature moved indoors": feathers, stones, rocks, sea shells, bones, seeds, pine cones, puppets, children's art, weavings with natural dyes, and her own wonderful pottery in evidence everywhere. Pictures of family also hang in abundance: five children and two grandchildren, as well as photographs of flowers and vegetables, all products of Sue's enormous gardens. In this house in High Falls, things now are "tidied up." The shells are contained in a glass jar, the rocks collected in baskets—the feel is different—less random, and I know it is because recently Sue's only daughter came to live with her. While all the pieces are still there, they've been tamed some.

I ask Sue to search for the artifacts of her teaching life that she has mentioned over the months of our taping together. She disappears into a closet and then digs in a file cabinet and the pieces begin to appear. With Sue and with Mona, I sometimes have the feeling that I am working on a huge jigsaw puzzle with so many pieces. Sometimes, due to so many elapsed years between the event and the recalling of it, it is difficult to be exact. I find myself trying different pieces that almost fit, but can't be forced into the space I'm trying to fill. I have to be patient, keep looking, keep trying to find the right piece. And then there are those moments when one finds a piece and it slips neatly and smoothly into place—like Prince Charming sliding the glass slipper onto Cinderella's foot.

Sue brings some of the pieces to me this morning: a resume, a philosophy statement, an article published in *Learning* magazine (February 1973) about her "open classroom" at Bank Street, a filmstrip and record made of her work there, letters from students she taught years ago, an article she authored for Scholastic's *Early Childhood Today* (February 1994). I get the feeling I had at Mona's when my pulse begins to race a little—the picture that the puzzle eventually will be, takes on a little more focus.

We go out for lunch and find ourselves in a bookstore. I find her standing in front of the books on tape section. Something clicks for me and I think back to the many evening and mornings I've had at Sue's—or even awakened in the middle of the night—to hear her listening to tapes. It is not now, because she is in her eighties and may have some difficulty reading. It has always been so and I think that she perhaps learns best by hearing. Home again, I examine the pile next to her bed containing tapes on life and living and learning and growing—spiritual and physical—Deepak Chopra, Bernie Siegel, Jean Houston, and Joseph Campbell. When I pull her books off the shelf, there is rarely any evidence of her engagement there. She does not underline, annotate, or make marks in the margins. I occasionally find a slip of paper marking a spot. Downstairs there is a nearly floor-to-ceiling cabinet with tapes. She says she listens again and again—the voices that instruct and nurture her, learning and relearning.

At night, sitting next to a fire, her daughter reads the Burpee seed catalogs. In this snowy weather, they are harbingers that there will yet be another spring. Sue is reading *Conversations with God* and I am sampling *Women's Ways of Knowing*.

A week later, I am back home looking out the window at the tops of trees. I have been looking at them all week. "Strange," I'm thinking, "46 years and yet I never took notice of the very tips." I often have admired the winter silhouettes of bare trees, loved the patterns they etch against a changing sky, and yet I never noticed how each tree's tips are so different: Some stretch straight and narrow, some curve like clawed hands, some grow plump with promise.

On a walk the week before, Sue and I had been admiring them. "Oh yes, I love them," I'd said quickly, when she mentioned the trees. "Yes," she said, "but *look* how the *tips* do just so." When Sue told me in an earlier taping about her mother's art classes that she used to sit in on, she said, "She was teaching me to *see*!" It is a gift she has tried to pass on.

On the way back from that walk, our path followed a river. "I guess the nice thing about a river is you always feel it's going somewhere; it's not stuck in some dead end," Sue says. And I think that this is how I have known her to live her life. Always going somewhere, no matter how old she grows, taking note of new things and helping others see old things anew.

CHAPTER 7

The Very Public Private Studio: An Examination of Craft

Those first 3 days are the hardest. Steep trails and deep ravines. Loose rock on the trail bed. At dusk the wind carries on a conversation with the trees. You stop along the way to write in fit and starts. You've begun this journey now, and your backpack is full to overflowing with the provisions stocked from the advice from earlier chapters. Now, it is important to explore the best ways to represent this work through the writing. On the morning of the fourth day, you reach a stream, and there is an old woman humming a song you almost recognize. She takes one look at you and wags her head. "Come now! Hurry."

It's the sound of voices you hear first. A band saw whines against the grain of wood. You see the rock foundation of a house perched on a hillside. The woman opens a large wooden door. You did not expect to find small groups gathered at tables or stretched out on long couches. You can barely find room to walk among them, their yellow legal pads, computers, and stacks of books. Littering the floor are stacks of pages with revision after revision, hand markings on printed pages. People are sitting next to each other, some deep in thought, others reading.

"Didn't I hear the sounds of wood working?" you ask the old woman.

She takes your arm and looks you right in the eyes. "Yes, they are working the whorls of wood," she tells you, "into the particulars of life."

There is a sign above the fireplace: "A writer's most valuable tools are memory and the senses." As you look more closely, you recognize some of the faces around bistro tables. "Listen," says Winterson (1995), "what is visible, the finished books, are underpinned by the fertility of uncounted hours" (p. 17). Stegner (2002) nods, "The best times I know are the times when some raw crystal of experience, my own or something I have observed, is being ground down and faceted and polished so that it reflects light and meaning" (p. 121). And, Oates (2004) pauses a moment before adding, "*I have to tell* is the writer's first thought; the second thought is *How do I tell it*? From our reading, we discover how various the solutions to these questions are; how stamped with an individual's personality. For it's at the juncture of private vision and the wish to create a communal, public vision that art and craft merge" (p. 126). While each of these writers expresses the work of craft differently, they each speak from the very center of individual experience in this very public private workshop.

You turn toward the sound of a familiar voice. David is reading a passage aloud to Ruth from an early draft of a dissertation in which the writer describes students' participation in a literature circle: "*In their individual discussions, engagement was not very high.*" David says, "You know, he's generally a good writer, but here he's telling us and not showing us, not making that classroom come alive. Wouldn't it be fair to say the point is to give the reader a sense of really being there? Let us see and hear the lack of engagement."

David hands the manuscript to Ruth, a 40-page chapter that appears to be a series of statements about the student and teacher interaction. "Here's another example." Ruth reads: "*Three of the students don't seem involved in their small group discussion. It appears they haven't read the assigned chapters. Miss Burris doesn't seem affected by this. She keeps her focus on other students.*"

David nods, "This writing does not provide the details that lead the reader to understand where a statement such as *the students don't seem involved* or *they haven't read the assigned chapters* comes from. How do we come to trust the interpreter of events here?"

Ruth sets the dissertation aside: "The distinctions in narrative research between a description and interpretation and between data and analysis, aren't entirely clear-cut. Is it even possible to create a 'data section' in narrative inquiry where you tell what happens and you don't narrate through showing? Isn't the narrating itself an act of revealing interpretation?"

David looks back at the sentence stating that students weren't involved. "I'm making this up, but go with me here. Something like:

Chandra stares out the window when Amelia asks the group if they felt sorry for the character. Chris preoccupies himself by punching the keypad on his calculator. Amelia looks around for someone to respond. Gregory puts his head on his desk. Three out of the five students in this group do not pick up their novels or attempt to respond to Amelia's question. The interpretation is present and clear in the descriptions."

Ruth responds, "This example is a good way to begin this chapter about narrative crafting and the forms and strategies a writer can use to increase verisimilitude and degrees of interpretation in accordance with their study's purpose."

David continues, "We might suggest that our readers look around this writers' workshop/studio and take a closer look at the crafting writers engage in. Let's encourage them to pause at the tables and work benches, open the drawers to the archives of examples of writers showing their revision processes, where we see examples of imagery, pacing, figurative language, and other resources of language. Many gather in this studio to study forms, rhetorical and literary devices, organizational structures, and other resources that are agents of representation, interpretation, and production of narratives."

THE CRAFT BEHIND NARRATIVES COMES TO LIGHT

Later that evening, you come to a large room where people interested in narrative research gather. Jen takes a seat between Ruth and David on the couch. Her brows narrow, and the three of them inhale, awaiting her question. "I have one last paper in my qualitative analysis class, and the professor suggested I write the methodology section for a narrative inquiry I want to do for my dissertation research. I've read about narrative inquiry and the theory behind it, but when I read narrative research methods texts, I haven't found anything where the methodology is narrated. What do I do?"

Ruth looks to David then back to Jen. "Oh, perfect! Well, we were just writing and talking about this very thing today! In this chapter we highlight narrative devices and techniques that writers have available to them in making decisions about how to present their narrative research."

Whether storying methodology, constructing narratives, or providing interpretations and analysis, the writing necessitates an awareness of the crafting resources available for writers. Careful consideration of craft requires awareness of how language, punctuation, sentence structure, or organization creates immediacy, controls pacing, replicates conversations through dialogue, or creates a strong sense of time and place. What point of view makes sense? What is the best way to organize time sequences? What are effective ways to bring a scene to life? We learn how craft and meaning work "in relation" one to the other. While authors may not always talk about this directly, reading narratives with an eye toward writing, as we suggested in Chapter 2, is part of the ongoing process of learning about craft. Some authors share their craft choices in metafiction or occasionally through interviews, so searching these out is an important part of the work as well.

Buy several books that focus specifically on craft (Burroway, 2010; Gerard, 1998; Hills, 2000; Martin, 2005) for your reference shelf. Have a trusted friend or small reading group that will read your work and focus on the effect of your crafting decisions. While it is true that there is a strong relationship between the theories of narrative that appeal to you and the craft elements you will want to use, it is important to recognize that you must experiment with forms and devices before you can easily articulate exactly how these affect meaning and presentation.

AN INVITATION TO EXPERIMENT

We suggest you write your way to understanding craft by experimenting through writing. As we demonstrate how various narrative strategies control perspective and interpretation, we invite you to try these out to learn about the myriad effects. For example, how might descriptions of the play of light and sound in a classroom replicate the atmosphere felt in that environment? Or, how might the noise and movement in a classroom be described only through dialogue, and what effect would this choice have on how the classroom is portrayed? How might you describe a classroom vibrant with learning and joy? What colors from your palette will prove most effective? Crafting is part of the serious work of writing compelling narratives that reveals aspects of the subjective experiences of participants and the researcher.

Before we get too far, we encourage you to track the choices you consciously make, to journal them in order to share the details of your crafting choices, to story your crafting decisions in the same ways you narrate the theoretical and methodological journeys within your research. These reflections will provide important insights for your readers regarding the dilemmas you confronted, and will aid others preparing to embark on their own research voyages. Most often, a discussion of decision making pertaining to a research study is placed in a single section of a methods chapter or in a discussion of role of the researcher, as we discussed in Chapter 2 with metanarratives. While these choices may make sense for a particular purpose, we believe these metanarrative discussions are most effective when woven into the fabric of the narrative research text.

We designed the chapters in this book to follow this approach. We reveal our motivations and struggles in narrative; take you, our readers, on a journey through narrative; create the dialogue that goes on between us; illustrate with other narrative examples; and bring other researchers and writers into the conversation.

We ask you even as David is right now asking Jen and the seminar group gathered in the workshop, "What types of stories most appeal to you? Do you like Dickensian details with explosive colors? Are you partial to Carver-esque minimalism, with perhaps more subtle tones? Do you appreciate endings neat and resolved, with clear moral conclusions, or do you prefer open-ended, O'Henry-type endings, filled with questions and complexity?"

And you and all those gathered in the seminar room, inside the writers' studio, somewhere deep in the woods of thought and contemplation, go on well into the night writing, talking about writing, and reading. Now, David tells you, "It's time to get to work and think through some of the specific resources we have available to us."

TEMPORALITY: THE TIME MACHINES OF NARRATIVE

Time is a blind guide.

Bog boy, I surfaced into the miry streets of the drowned city. For over a thousand years, only fish wandered Biskupin's wooden sidewalks. Houses, built to face the sun, were flooded by the silty gloom of the Gasawka River. Gardens grew luxurious in subaqueous silence; lilies, rushes, stinkweed.

No one is born just once. If you're lucky, you'll emerge again. . . .

—Michaels, 1998, p. 5

Once Upon a Time. Dickens's "It was the best of times, it was the worst of times." Flashforward, flashback; the next morning, 17 years ago. We live in and out of time, time collapses and expands, time becomes elastic, we move through time—all this we can do reading in our armchairs or writing at our desks.

The uses of time in narrative inquiry are important for sequencing, providing chronology, and demonstrating the strong relationships among past, present, and future. Stories, Aristotle suggested, are characterized as a form by containing a beginning, middle, and end. But our experiences tell us life doesn't fit so neatly into a narrative sequence. Given that a beginning is somewhat arbitrary for any story, what decisions need to be made to determine where to start? For example, what happened in a classroom before a researcher started a study there, and what histories do the students bring with them that are an important part of the narrative that needs telling? What futures tug them through their daily existence?

Chronological order is not always the best way to organize because it might not highlight aspects of the narrative that require a reader's attention. Are flashbacks useful along the way, and how are decisions made about where and why to include them? Are there intersecting tales that should be stitched together in some fashion? Maybe beginning *in medias res* at the point of crisis or joy serves to make a particular point, that is, what anthropologists might call an *emblematic tale*. Knowing the repertoire of narrative resources to manipulate and control the temporal aspects of narrative gives the researcher choices to make, and those choices can be determined only by the particular ways in which individual narrative research studies unfold.

Considerations of Time: A Demonstration

Back in the seminar room, Ryan asks, "Could you give us a concrete example of temporality to work through? You were telling us the other night about going back to teach a high school class in addition to your university teaching. Could you give us some examples of how time might factor into how you would narrate the research?"

"Yes, let's do that." David says. "I might start writing: *The School of Social Justice—we call it SOJO—is on the west side of Chicago, in Little Village. There, I co-taught a creative writing class with Angela, a graduate of our English education program.* That sounds a little like a Once Upon a Time start!" David laughs.

Jen pushes David to give another example. "It sounds really cool, a school focused on social justice teaching. How will the way you order time be influenced by what was learned from the experience?"

"If I order chronologically I might stress how the experience is a roller coaster ride of ups and downs. As with any teaching, it's great one day and really challenging the next." David draws a timeline on the whiteboard. "You would have a rendering of successful social jus- tice work one day and miserable failure another, and several other more mundane days in between." David marks out an even number of weeks on the timeline and makes a little graph marking the high and low spots. "If I want to emphasize what I learned *over time* then chronology may still be important. So, I could create a timeline of how my thinking changed over the months I taught there.

"If I don't organize chronologically, I could organize *chunks of time*—one chunk might bring together all the important lessons I learned across the months. Another chunk might emphasize the confusions across those months. In this case the chronology doesn't matter." David erases the timeline to make his point.

"I teach courses on social justice work at UIC, so I can imag- ine *juxtaposing time* and maybe move back and forth between what happens in the high school class and the discussions we had in my university classes. Those leaps away from a literal time sequence between the high school and university could definitely emphasize how we talk about this work in theory in universities and how it plays out in the high school." David draws two big boxes on the whiteboard and labels one UIC and the other SOJO, and draws squiggly lines to connect events that correspond.

"To emphasize this, I could start my narrative by writing: *I have not done day-to-day high school teaching for decades! I'm team teaching with Angela, starting off with poetry, and for some students it seems to work right from the get-go. We are writing out of our lives and experiences and some kids like it. However, many students don't come to class with the assigned work, and others put their heads down and sleep or stare out the window or chat with friends.* Then, I could have flashbacks to my own earlier high school teaching in rural Hudsonville as I work with these students." David erases the boxes that demonstrated juxtaposition and draws a timeline with flashback balloons along it. "What might the combination of chronology and flashbacks emphasize?"

Another member of the seminar suggests that David's earlier teaching might inform how he works with the current students. "Now, imagine I want to start my narrative *in medias res*. I'd probably start with a story from the third day because it sets the scene for much of what happens."

> Michael complains, "Schaafsma! We HATE this poetry, man."
>
> I say, "Michael, it's an elective class in creative writing, you're a senior; what did you think the class was going to be about?"
>
> "I don't know!"
>
> "Well, what do you want to do instead?"
>
> "Nothing!"

Everyone laughs at this familiar student answer.

David suggests, "This version only makes one student come alive, but it might be one attempt to set into motion what the next months will be like. Now, let me tell the story a different way. I'll focus on curricular events, and let's think about how time is organized here and what is emphasized."

> We had poetry readings to honor Illinois war dead; we did a unit on Chicago Public School kids killed in the past 2 years called The Backpack Project, in part set up by some Quakers who came in to our school; kids read poems at Daley Plaza downtown with reporters present and TV news cameras running.

Here time collapses into major happenings. Whole months collapse into single sentences. There aren't details or individual students here. What is happening in the classroom that undermines the broadly happy version of events isn't present. In the day-to-day experiences, we end up kicking out kids on a weekly basis for being disruptive, for saying things or throwing stuff. Many of these kids just want to get out of the school and graduate. It's ironic that in spite of the school's noble social justice aims, these teenagers still express restlessness and wildness. Some of this could be told through flashbacks.

Throughout this seminar, it becomes clear how important it is for a researcher to think carefully about how to organize, manage, and slow down or speed up time in order to emphasize particular aspects of a study.

> The past still lives in us . . . has made us what we are and is remaking us every moment! . . . An hour is not merely an hour. It is a vase filled with perfumes, sounds, places and climates! . . . So we hold within us a treasure of impressions, clustered in small knots, each with a flavor of its own, formed from our own experiences, that become certain moments of our past. (Proust, 1982, p. 127)

WHERE THERE IS VISION: POINT OF VIEW

> *Meet in expensive beige raincoats, on a pea-soupy night. First, stand in front of Florsheim's Fifty-seventh Street window, press your face to the glass, watch the fake velvet Hummels inside. You can see your breath on the glass. Draw a peace sign. You are waiting for a bus.*
>
> —Moore, 2007, p. 3

Point of view is the lens through which experiences of the narrative are filtered. Readers hear and see only through the narrator's perspective, but multiple narrators complicate any one, simple reading. A common assignment in English classes for seeing from another's perspective is to rewrite a section of a story from another character's point of view. A change in the person telling a story, or a change from where the person tells the story, makes all the difference in what gets told. Who speaks for whom, and why and to what effect? There are important political and ideological considerations on who is given privilege to speak in research narratives and how the narrators are portrayed through the perspective they offer.

Let's imagine how Michael might see David:

> This old White dude comes into our classroom now every day to teach with Ms. Sangha. He comes down the hall all smiling at us like he actually likes it here, and trying to do fist bumps and all that, trying to make out like he is street, which is kinda funny. He has us do all this poetry stuff: forms and crap. We just

write and write all the time just like every other class so it's nothing special like they said it was supposed to be. It's just like every
other thing in this place: BORING.

David tells this story: "Michael, a few days after he said he didn't
want to write poetry, actually did read a poem he wrote about the
passing of his grandmother. He's a big guy, tears just running down
both cheeks and some of us who hear it are crying, too. So of course if
I want to bring him alive and complicate my rendering of him I need
to include his poem; I need excerpts from interviews with him so
readers can hear what he is thinking about in his own words. I would
have loved the opportunity to co-write with him, something similar
to what Fleischer (1995) did with her research participants in the last
chapter of her book about a composition class."

How present do you want to be in the research story you tell?
Are there studies in which muting your personal voice or presence
would be advantageous or truthful? Might the effect be a greater focus on others whom you are telling stories about? How much of your
life and perspective needs to get identified if your narrative research
topic focuses on student projects in another teacher's classroom?

Jen says, "I see. In order to narrate this methodology I should talk
about choices like that."

Ruth responds. "We've often privileged first-person stories in our
text—for instance, 'Take hold of the fact that *you* are telling a story'—
but we recognize there are myriad points of view available. Consider
how we use second person in this book. We made a conscious decision to have our readers as a character in this book because as we see
it our readers are on the narrative research journey with us."

Melanie adds, "McInerney (1997) uses second person throughout
his novel, *Bright Lights, Big City*. The effect seems a kind of welcom-
ing, a kind of enfolding the reader in a shared venture. *You* are there."

Ruth adds, "But deciding on the person to tell the story is only
one level of decision making in determining who will narrate your
research projects. Will the narrator recognize and involve the reader
directly, challenge the reader to be part of the narrative? If so, why?"

Dave breaks in, "If an incident in the classroom is best explained
by revealing a conversation with the teachers that provides personal
and possibly painful information, who should narrate that story?

Who chooses the exact words? Who decides if it is too much to tell? How much of your reaction should be revealed? How do you position yourself in the narrative so you don't completely take it over? How present do you need to be?"

"Yes!" Ruth adds. "Questions like these are related to the degree of omniscience in the narrating of the research story. Perspectival closeness or distance—what I call 'psychic distance,' or what Mark Currie (1998) refers to as the 'mobility' of the narrator (p. 97)—provides us with another resource that allows us to filter perspective in multiple ways. How close do you want to be as narrator to the subjects of your story? How much do you want your readers to know about the subjects' less-than-admirable qualities? Can we imagine a subject's thoughts? Can we know several subjects' thoughts?"

David continues, "Part of our concern about psychic space and distance pertains to the question of whether I will telephoto to the footsie being played under the desks by Miguel and Ayanna as they work on poems in response to a reading of Giovanni's *My House* (1972) about new love. Is it somehow voyeuristic, or the perfect detail, or both?"

ARE YOU SURE ABOUT THAT?
NARRATOR RELIABILITY AND TRUSTWORTHINESS

I get the willies when I see closed doors. Even at work, where I am doing so well now, I can almost smell the disaster mounting invisibly and flooding out toward me through the frosted glass panes. My hands may perspire and my voice may come out strange. I wonder why. Something must have happened to me sometime.

—Heller, 1997, p. 3.

Jen brought it up after everyone shared writing from point-of-view explorations. "It seems like point of view is related to issues of reliability, no? Such as: At what point do we need to get to know certain people better than others, and to what extent can we trust the narrator or narrators in the depiction of such details? What are responsible ways to make those decisions?"

"And, of course," Ruth adds, "we can never know what isn't said, what ideas are swept under the rug of circumstance or desire or just not noticing. At what point do we feel it is responsible to surmise what others are thinking or feeling (as David did in inventing thoughts for Michael) or is this crossing an interpretive/ethical line? At what point might such a move weaken your reliability as a narrator? Is the omniscient—sometimes referred to as the *God's eye*—point of view a tenable or believable narrator stance for narrative researchers?"

All narrators are ultimately unreliable since perspective is always limited, but the task for a narrator/speaker includes convincing readers of reliability, sincerity, commitment to fairness, and honesty. Researchers employ strategies such as triangulation of data, involving various stakeholders in interpreting or analyzing the data, verifying this with the stamp of approval of a university institutional review board (IRB), complete with signed copies of human subject permission slips, but in narrative inquiry the subject of narrator reliability necessitates subtle and careful crafting decisions.

Dave reminds the group, "So we are all unreliable narrators. We all invent the past to some extent as we tell stories of our lives."

Gregory says, "True, but narrators can actually gain credibility and reliability through admissions of fallibility, as Greg Michie (2009) does when he speaks of all the mistakes he makes as a teacher in his story of his teaching career."

"Probably! Well, let's go back to the SOJO example and look at how a layering of unreliable narrators has impact on the research story. You already have some glimpses of Michael from my perspective, and how I imagine Michael sees me. Now, here's another perspective, what a journalist said to me at the Daley Plaza."

From David's Field Notes (October 4, 2009)

> Oh, you teach in Latino Village? I grew up on the south side. These kids are not all bad but they sort of want to be, they have this pressure to be bad, and that's the truth. They can't do the work, they can't read, they can't write, they feel inadequate, they want something to make them feel good about themselves, so you give them a gun and they bad. They killahs. All these kids are this way; I grew up there, I know.

David asks: "What's your take on this person's perspective? How do you make decisions about how reliable his perspective might be?

Do you trust him? Layering multiple narrators' versions is sometimes useful in narrative inquiry to help the reader recognize that reliability of a single narrator cannot be assumed."

"This is a version of a letter of apology written by a group of boys for something they had done in class." David makes certain everyone in the seminar has a copy. "The group of boys understood that the teacher, Angela, could get them suspended for their actions, so the principal demanded a written apology. See what this letter tells you about the boys and how they are depicted by what they say."

Dear Mr. Rodriguez, Ms. Sangha, and Mr. Schaafsma,

We apologize for our offensive actions in Ms. Sangha's classroom. We did not mean to disrespect any girls by using "D' Ridin'" signs. We was just playing like we do in our neighborhood, and having fun, not wanting to hurt nobody. If you would watch closely you would see that the girls also use these signs but they call it "P' Ridin'" and this does not make us mad and we don't think they are mad at us, either. Sometimes we just use these signals just like throwing up the middle finger and it doesn't mean sex or something bad for girls, it just is fun or could be angry in some cases but isn't always meant to be putting down other people. Please don't suspend us from school; we would get in a lot of trouble with our parents and we think it is an extreme punishment for this crime.

We are very sorry,
Michael, Antwon, Demann, and Marquis

Take a few minutes, now, and think through the various perspectives provided here. What do the students reveal about themselves? What is the tone of the letter? Do you believe them? What, in their own language or in what you learned about them from others, "rings true" here? These are the types of questions we grapple with and that we must write into our narrative research.

We believe the goal of all stories is to be persuasive and compelling, but at the same time, open to questioning. Think carefully now: Who is the narrator (or narrators) who will tell the stories within your narrative inquiry? How will you provide accounts of the background of narrators in order to provide enough information for your reader to make judgments on reliability? How might layered stories and multiple narrators assist you in presenting reliable and trustworthy stories?

"Go sleep on those questions," Ruth suggests. "David and I will see you in the morning."

You walk out on the porch, wrap yourself in a quilt, open your notebook, and begin to write.

Who Are These People and How Did They Get Here?

Fifteen years ago she had gone under. It was nothing you could put your finger on; there had been no scene, no snap; only the slow-sinking, water-logged, of her will into his.
—Woolf, 2008, p. 13

"So how do you develop characters?" Riley asks. Everyone has gathered after breakfast to continue the seminar.

David suggests, "The main characters, the central 'informants,' need to be fleshed out more than the minor characters, but what kind of telling details are necessary? Let's look at these questions by taking a close look at Michael again, from my notes."

Michael is 18, African American, with short cropped hair, standing maybe 6'3", 250 pounds, and physically imposing, though he also has a sweet smile when he wants to use it. Multiple labels mark him via special education, and he's out of class as much as he is in; he's a wannabe rap artist that has to be told to take the headphones off multiple times a day. He glowers at you when you tell him to sit down, class is beginning, and then, maybe, or maybe not, he grins as if to say, "I'm just playin', Mr. S," as he slides into his seat.

"What do you learn about Michael here and what is important to know?" David asks. "Do we need to know he is African American, or that he is physically 'imposing'—and to whom?—or has short hair? Is the glowering balanced out by the grinning, as if to say 'he's tough, but can be sweet'? If he is 'multiply labeled' is it problematic to share this, and what do you gain or lose by not naming the specific labels? Maybe the headphones are enough to make the point that Michael can be a challenge."

Ruth adds, "And what gives any of us the right to tell anything about him, really? Should he be speaking for himself? At what point do researchers become guilty of sensationalism or romanticism, especially when they write about populations historically stereotyped by the media and the academy?"

Just how is character or personality revealed? Is it through dress, gestures, hair style? We think one of the key ways character is revealed is through speech, and dialogue, and as we see it, one of the failings of much research is that it reports speech rather than lets us listen in.

Pastiche:
Hybridity, Layered Stories, Collage, and Multigenre

When everyone gathers again after lunch, the conversation moves to the question of how to structure multiple viewpoints.

"Structural and organizational concerns are addressed more fully in the book that Ruth co-authored [Ely et al. (1997)]. Let's highlight some of what we have been suggesting about multivocality and multiplicity, but we recommend you read that book," David suggests.

Ely and colleagues (1997) consider the effects of multiplicity, where two or more perspectives, themes, or ideas produce something new or engender multiple contexts for the data in order "to yield different avenues of insight with the purpose of challenging, mixing, testing, and ultimately transgressing what the researcher or reader knows" (p. 40). Ely and colleagues speak of the idea of multiplicity itself as a *conceptual prism*, a more fluid and dynamic image than a simple mirror image. If we think of multiple perspectives in terms of simply lining them up or listing them in some sort of static fashion, one after the other, then the notion of a prism held up to the light, and always changing every moment, encourages us to invent ways to enact this in narrative.

Most research reports, including many narratives, tend to "smooth" out the data to create the illusion of one clear view. We suggest you consider interrupting that clarity through some of the resources that narrative offers. Think of the prism as a way to show dimensions of puzzlement, confusion, or roadblocks.

The advantages of the pastiche include that multiple data sources interact simultaneously and that it provokes questions more than represents reality. Data might be taken from conversations, journals, interviews, or artifacts of any kind, but pastiche is built on intertextuality. "Each text acts on the other so that *texture* results. The effect is kinetic, giving a dynamic quality and a sense of immediacy as the separate pieces deliver new meaning, at times complementary and at others contradictory" (Ely et al., 1997, p. 100). Some interesting examples from literacy research include Vielstimmig (1999).

David asks those gathered in the seminar: "Are there models from literature you can suggest for crafting pastiche?" Riley mentions Silko's *Ceremony* (2006); Gregory recommends Ondaatje's *The Collected Works of Billy the Kid* (2004); Ruth can't resist adding Momaday's *The Way to Rainy Mountain* (1969), which combines story, myth, and historical accounts to interweave various types of knowledge.

The structures grow out of ways to organize the mingling of various forms and perspectives. We think of braiding, weaving, for instance, as metaphors for structural choices. Braiding your researcher voice with student voices, for example, might be an interesting possibility. We admit that narratives that operate in this way may be difficult for some readers, but in our view, they can be exciting and more reflective of the existence of simultaneity than other, more conventional narratives.

FICTION, OR INVENTING THE TRUTH

> . . . in my idle afternoons I have imagined this story plot which I shall perhaps write some-day and which already justifies me somehow. Details, rectifications, adjustments are lacking; there are zones of the story not yet revealed to me; today, January 3rd, 1944, I seem to see it as follows: The action takes place in an oppressed and tenacious country: Poland, Ireland, or some South American state.
>
> —Borges, 1969, p. 27

"While we are talking about artful versions of experience," Ruth suggests, "I'd love to see us talk about fiction as educational research."

"Well," David says, "In studies dealing with sensitive subjects such as rape, we know that 'composite' subjects with fictional contexts are created to preserve anonymity. This is a time-honored practice in many disciplines."

Jen said, "I admire the ways fictional narratives in novels and films represent classrooms and communities, so why not try these ourselves?"

We particularly appreciate the work of Clough (2002), who creates fictions as part of his research on schools and families. "Data," he says, "may have to be manipulated to tell the truth as one sees it" (p. 17). Fiction involves acts of imagination, invention, construction; all language involves these acts, but fiction consciously does so.

"But how do you assess it?" Riley asks. "We have agreed upon standards for criteria for other forms of research. What might they be for fictional research?"

David suggests, "Maybe the questions are different for stories and fiction: Have these stories moved, touched, or taught us? Are they useful, believable, interesting? Are they generative of readers' stories on related topics? You can assess fictional research according to the standards of any story: degree of engagement and aesthetic standards, verisimilitude and authenticity, and ethical considerations such as integrity."

It's an important ethical issue when a researcher claims something has happened but doesn't tell us it is really based on a distant memory or fiction, as opposed to field notes from a research journal. But we worry, too, that sometimes field notes may take on the aura of fact, when perception may be flawed and perspective obscured. Geertz (1998) claims that all anthropological data bear a close relationship to fiction; in fact the epistemological distinctions between them are too slippery to be useful. Tim O'Brien (1990) talks about the advantages of "story-truth" over "happening-truth" for the purpose of capturing reality.

"Even if we acknowledge what Geertz and O'Brien are saying," Ruth says, "the important issue for educational research is how these fictional stories relate to the experienced realities of the classroom."

"Right," Gregory says. "Can we researchers 'make it all up,' and, if so, what's the ethical difference between these accounts and lies? Feels like murky water to be swimming in."

Howard Gardner and Elliot Eisner (Saks, 1996) debated whether novels might be dissertations. Eisner, art educator and artist, and then-president of the American Educational Research Association (AERA), was in favor of accepting the novel as an artistic form of scholarship; Gardner, in spite of his advocacy for multiple intelligences, was skeptical: "In novels you can say whatever you want, and you are judged by how effectively you say it without particular regard to truth value." Research, in Gardner's view, "is an effort to find out as carefully as you can and then to report it accurately" (p. 400). Eisner responded that issues of truth are not confined to science, but are often at the heart of fictional endeavors. He thought, in addition to being concerned with truthfulness and accuracy, that novels may "promote empathetic participation in the lives of others" (p. 408).

Gardner's concern was scientific accuracy, a goal that novels couldn't serve for him. Eisner didn't disagree, but he wanted to advocate for broader and more inclusive conceptions of truth in research. Gardner admitted that works of art might be beautiful and expressive but lacked "translatability" and a capacity "to be reduced to an additional brick of knowledge" (p. 411). Yet Goodman (1978) wrote, "The arts must be taken no less seriously than the sciences as modes of discovery, creation and the enlargement of knowledge in the broad sense of advancing human understanding" (p. 102).

David ends the seminar by reminding everyone that "engagement with the material becomes what makes the story compelling, not a cool rendering of the facts. This is one central consideration to keep in mind. Take some time now to write and think all this through."

Writing Your Way into the Inquiry

Jen returns a few days later with a draft that reflects some of her early thinking and meditation on the processes of beginning this work.

They are students from a small high school (student body: approximately 400) who were my students and the data are drawn from that time, their 9th-, 10th-, and 11th-grade years. The students are mostly African American and Latino/a. They attended high school in the poorest urban area in America, the South Bronx. They have a variety of abilities, they come from various perspectives on life, but mostly, they come from schools in which they have been underserved. Some sleep on mattresses in the kitchen with their grandmothers. Some wrestle between selling drugs and coming to class. Some refused to read, some don't read much, some didn't read at all. All of them deserve something better. This is why they deserve the voice of the study.

My participants are true co-authors in this study, and if I were smart enough to think of it, I would have allowed them to author it all by themselves. They are competent, capable children of the South Bronx, the ones whom people you know would label as "anti-intellectual." They are not. I make no claims of being separate from this story: I am deeply invested in who these children are and who they will become. They are strong, smart, and sensible young people. Before, during, and after I taught them, I heard from the people in my life that they surely must be none of the above; you must not believe those people, because they don't know.

I want to share them with you: our stories and our experiences, from the first day when Matthew offered to walk Tariq to the bathroom because Tariq was afraid of being eaten alive by the seniors, to the last day when Eddie, a self-declared illiterate whom no one thought would pass the RCTs much less the Regents, walked across that graduation stage smiling with every last tooth and waving a bona fide New York City high school diploma over his head while making the shape of the Bronx "X" with his arms. I am not unbiased; I am, instead, filled with bias: I want these beautiful students to be heard by everyone willing to listen and especially by those who aren't, I want every last one of them to get as much out of their potential-filled lives as the kids a mile away in Manhattan who get twice the money and twice the chance at a great life as my students get. I want their voices to matter as much as teacher voices, administrator voices.

"Yes," Dave says, "I'm starting to feel the presence of the kids. You obviously care about these kids and we can see from this ways you will begin shaping the narratives of your passion."

"I am? It's daunting, but exciting as well. I can see there is so much for me to try."

If this section from Jen feels like the beginning of a storying the journey, in the next chapter we return to a story we began in Chapter 6, from Randi Dickson, who stories the work of completing her dissertation. At each stage she made craft decisions, chiseling and stitching and honing her narrative inquiry.

CHAPTER 8

Dilemmas of Craft

RANDI DICKSON

In this chapter, Randi grapples with the processes and consequences of trying to (re)present a life through interviews and artifacts. She struggles with several questions: What is her role in the construction of narratives depicting a complex life? What and how does she story herself through the stories she tells of others? What are the ethics in depicting the frailties or difficulties encountered? Randi describes disappointment and frustration with her capacity to narrate the separate threads of complex lives. Ultimately, she wonders how to capture in words what is much like trying to grasp air and fog—the magic that is a life.

STORYING THE RESEARCHER

In Chapter 7, Dave and Ruth give us a rich palette to draw from as we plan the move from the gathering of data to the fashioning of the text. Many questions arise, presenting puzzles to be solved, and dilemmas—rhetorical, aesthetic, ethical—to wrestle with. Many of these can be fun (yes!), exploratory and playful in nature, creative in ways that can be exhilarating and deeply engaging. But some of our choices, particularly as our lives entwine with those of participants, can cause dilemmas we may not have anticipated.

In the following passages, drawn from my oral history research, I story the dilemmas of trying to do this work with someone who is removed by age and memory from the life I am trying to capture. How does one suggest that without diminishing the person who is or was, and without appropriating the tale? How much should one disclose of the problems the material might be presenting?

It is no small thing to be entrusted with the story of a life, and we must tend carefully to how we return that life to the teller through our words.

JOURNAL ENTRY, JANUARY 16, 1999

Last night at 3 A.M., I lay in bed unable to sleep. I was still trying to figure out the puzzle of writing about Mona, still tortured that none of the multiple drafts I had begun, had yet to feel right. Each I time I read them over I was puzzled. They lacked immediacy and engagement. They seemed dull when they should have been about radiance, writing about such a colorful bird.

Earlier this week, I had given up on "capturing the magic"—and, for a while I felt some relief—I'd go back to what she had to say in the nearly 250 pages of transcripts that I had from her alone—I'd stick with those words and I'd work out of them. I followed the path I had laid out for myself: I worked out of the transcripts, copying sections and writing observations between them. I winced at how much I was in these pages—I had talked a lot. I had tried to let her tell her story in her words, but my words seemed to be intruding.

Then last night, just before midnight, I read over the last few days' work. Once again, my heart sank. It was okay, it got at some aspects of her approach to teaching and learning, but once again, it still didn't feel right. For 2 hours I lay awake, watching the stars through my bedroom window winking at me, as I tried to think of a new plan, a new "What if?" "What if I tried it this way instead of that?"

But each "What if?" felt like a path I'd been down before. I got out of bed, tiptoed past my sleeping children, plugged in my laptop, and started to write.

"Listen, I want to tell you a story," I began again and again. But my throat closed on the words and I could not force them out.

STARTING OVER

I thought I could write about Mona first, but I have come back to write about her last. Perhaps I thought I knew her best and she seemed most immediate, having lived in my home for 5 weeks in the spring of 1997. I began, but after many months I became discouraged with the tone, overwhelmed with the amount of conversation that we had spoken and the boxes of artifacts I had collected, and afraid, most of all, that I was losing the magic that is so much of Mona. In a journal entry from May 1998, I hear my frustration and my fear:

> I am getting anxious again, feeling I haven't found my way in, not liking the "research" tone, somehow clinical, somehow los-ing Mona. I feel I need to dig in the box of artifacts I shipped home from Mona's. I pull out two things to listen to: a set of tapes of Jean Houston from a workshop she did on creation myths and a videotape on Albert Einstein. Mona has often spoken of Jean's influence on her thinking, although when I press her, it is not a linear thing that she can tell me. I ride around in my car listening to Jean's voice, thinking of Mona listening to Jean's voice—not surprised at the voice, the tone, the thoughts about the magic and mystery of our universe.
>
> Later in Canio's little bookstore I am looking for Terrence McNally's play *Masterclass*. I have recently heard him read an excerpt from it and I get excited, thinking, "I can use this in my dissertation." I find his play of the great opera singer Maria Callas and the teaching classes she held. I also find Alice Walker's book, *Everything We Love Can Be Saved*, and I buy it, liking the title, and from some vague memory of a reference to an essay she wrote on Cuba that is done in "pastiche." I am looking for models.
>
> In bed that night I read all of *Masterclass* and cannot find what I thought would fit. I put it aside and reach for the Walker book. Flipping through, I find a poem—"Reassurance"—"I must love the questions," she begins and it calms me a little.

"Anything we love can be saved," the title of Walker's book tells me. In writing about Mona, I am trying in some small way to pre-serve her, to "save" her. I had only questions as to how to "evoke" Mona and so in mid-July I stopped trying to write about her and went on to work on other parts of my dissertation, and to write about the other two women in my study. I have returned now, spiraled back, as Bateson (1994) has shown me, hoping that "my groping key" fits a little truer.

Going deeper, coding and correlating, reading and rereading, *focusing*, the vision can become narrow. What I was yet to learn was that it was not just Mona I needed to look at more broadly, but my place in the whole process.

Majoring in Mona

There is a mounting body of theory which shows how there is both an ethical and a methodological failure involved in not recognizing the role of the researcher in the construction of the narrative and the text. We need modes of writing which show the kind of scaffolding and stages that went into its building.

—Measor & Sikes, 1992, p. 212

One morning during the time that Mona visited, she came with me to my daughter Lila's class. Lila was then in second grade and her teacher had invited parents and friends to come in every Friday to read with the children. I had been going most of the winter and thought Mona would enjoy reading too and seeing Lila's class. When my participants and I got together later that spring, I told them about this experience.

I was thinking about what you said about that ripple effect that teaching can have, and, you know, Mona left eastern Long Island in 1980 and has returned now for the first time in 17 years and if we go anywhere in educational settings she gets mobbed, literally mobbed. I took her down to the elementary school to read in Lila's classroom, she was just going to sit and read with the students. Well, within minutes there were four teachers around us in that school. They came running up. "You're *the* Mona Dayton?!!" "Oh, my God!" People started to tell stories about being in Mona's classes at Southampton College. (Mona: It was wonderful!) This young man came up who teaches kindergarten, [and] he said to Mona, "You taught me in my first education class I was ever in. I left after that for a while and the reason I returned was because of that experience with you that first year." And another started to say, "My best classes were with you, remember . . .? We made fried bread, we did . . ." (M: They remembered these things!), and then another time we went to the middle school, where Emma is, and a whole other slew of teachers came in and they said, "We *majored* in Mona!" (interview, May 29, 1997).

People other than students who met or knew Mona were affected in similar ways. In sifting through a collection of artifacts from the time when she was one of five finalists for National Teacher of the Year in 1966, I found several letters from Jerry Burke, the head of the research team who had been sent from New York City by *Look* magazine to meet with Mona. Burke wrote that he "enjoyed my visit with you and consider it among the truly inspiring encounters of my 6 years of 'teacher hunting.' I insist that we make plans to meet again—in one way or another, for it is unthinkable to assume that our paths may not cross again." In another letter he referred to a colleague who also had visited her classroom: "Dan was caught in the same magic web that fascinated me. Congratulations, Mona! How does it feel to be the winner of the National Teacher of the Year Award?"

Looking back, part of my paralysis might have been trying to capture that magic. *"Can* I?" I thought. *"How* can I?" How does one "capture magic"? I wanted to enable my readers to *know* that magic too. I wanted to *evoke* her in ways that literally would make her materialize. Anything less than that, I feared, would diminish her. I should have listened to my own warning as I quoted from Patti Lather (1991): "As I write, I face the inescapability of reductionism. Language is delimitation, a strategic limitation of possible meanings" (p. xix). For finally, I have found, I cannot. I cannot represent, evoke, or re-create Mona with words on a page, whether they're her words or my words or those of any who might pay tribute to her, or by pictures, or by any of the other artifacts that I produce to bear witness. I have learned that I never should have thought I could.

So I am left wondering what it might be possible to do instead. I have gone back, for the moment, to her telling of her life story. Rather than interrupting that with passages from other interviews as I initially experimented with, I have found once again that I must honor the "whole." I have found that I have to go back to the beginning, to her birth. So I begin there, with her life, in her words.

In Conversation

My dilemma as a researcher is to reconstruct and critically re-present the voices of others, and, in so doing, care for their integrity, humanity, and struggles.
                                                              —Britzman, 1991, p. 12

When Mona came to visit me in the spring of 1997, she arrived on the day before her 81st birthday. She had not been back to the east end of Long Island, where she lived and worked for 13 years, since she'd retired in 1980. I sent her a letter asking her to be part of my dissertation studies, and more, asking if she would come and stay with me so we could talk and I could tape our conversations. She not only came, but stayed nearly 5 weeks; we taped a last interview in the car on the way to Newark Airport. In that one, she finally talks at least as much as I do, as I was occupied (luckily) with driving. When I looked back at all of the transcripts of our conversations before that, I was amazed (and dismayed) by how much *I* talked.

It is clear in the transcripts how some of this happened and it is indicative of something about Mona. Throughout our interviews, she regularly turned the discussion or question back to me—"So how would you do it, Randi?" "What did you do?"—and perhaps too frequently, I bit the bait. I entered into the discussions with many of my own experiences and theories so that our sessions became much more conversations than interviews. When I saw how long my passages were, I regretted that I didn't learn the same technique from her sooner, as it is only in this conversation in the car that I finally say, "Oh, I'm not going to answer that. *I'm* not the one being interviewed!" I regretted it, although pushing me to form my own opinions and extend my thinking has been an important aspect of our time together throughout the years.

When David Schaafsma and Ruth Vinz, my advisors throughout this work, read earlier drafts of the chapter on Mona, they commented on the degree to which I am present. Ruth wrote, "You'll need to account for *your* part in the conversation." And David, reflecting in the margin of one portion of a transcript, wrote:

> Randi, [you're] filling in the testimony—*your* connections, or a kind of (Bahktin) ventriloquism—you're exhibiting [what] *you*

learned. They were your mentors, and *taught* you, so you're saying it back now in (sort of) recitation fashion! It's a kind of "active listening," or flattering echo, your interview technique.

And in another section of a transcript, where I elaborated on something Mona and I were discussing, he wrote, "Here, again, you extend the idea she has with more detail than she has given." Often those details are recollections of conversations we've had at other times in our lives or experiences I had visiting her classroom, as in this sample from a transcript:

> Like how you always used to say, [that] you'd always ask the
> kids, well, what did *they* know, how could they share it? and so,
> we all learn from people . . .

However, I have come to realize that there is another issue at work in the conversations we taped for this study. It is a realization that has been painful for me to see. Ruth said, "You'll need to account for your part. . . ." I see now that I tried to avoid "accounting"; instead, I looked for explanations that would support who and what I wanted to present—the woman and teacher I knew nearly 20 years ago. I can see now that I also talk so much because sometimes I am prompting Mona's thoughts and recollections. In some cases, that is because Mona is not sure what she wants to say; in other places, she has trouble recollecting the specifics of a situation, as most of us might if we were trying to remember things that happened many years ago. She often says, "I'm not sure, I don't remember," or "I think I might have . . ."

As I had promised, when I finished the draft of her profile, I sent it to her for verification. When it was returned to me—by her daughter—it came with a letter. At the time, I dismissed much of what it had to say, because I was bent on my mission—to "capture" the Mona we all had known. But in recent days, as I have struggled to discover why I seemed unable to construct a text that had Mona's words at the center, I have had to take a different look—the peripheral one that takes into account other factors. In part, what her daughter wrote, after helping Mona edit the profile, was that she was concerned that her mother's "methods would be trivialized" if I were unable to re-create in a vital way Mona's classroom and her reasons for teaching as she did. She expressed concern that Mona might no longer "have the words" to recollect all the wonderful things that made her the teacher who "taught students to be more than they thought they could, the teacher who turned people on to the excitement of learning, the witch on the broomstick who made you believe in magic, if just for a moment" (letter, March 1998).

So once again I am stepping back, trying to see what is possible now. I cannot do all that I set out to do. It has been hard letting go of that. The work is not a coherent whole; it does not present as smooth a narrative as I feel I was able to construct with Sue or Grace. The text I craft will be as much my words as it is Mona's—perhaps for many reasons. It will, I hope, give you a glimpse into the Mona that was, as well as the one that is still creating herself, as Bateson says, once again in how she remembers.

CHAPTER 9

Mind the Gaps

NICK SOUSANIS

Once Upon A Time . . . we imagined a concluding chapter titled "A Fable For the Future." This heady Fable would offer a 2030 narrative version of the field. That idea sent our imaginations speeding down the highway, but we veered off the road when we went around the first curve and ran head-on into Nick's graphic explorations. We were confronted by the fact that narratives are messy, composed of nested, overlapping elements, running in a multitude of directions simultaneously. The best way to end this book was to invite Nick to show rather than tell something of that future.

Comics are a language of juxtapositions, particularly well-suited to convey a richness and depth of non-linear, multi-layered narratives. By holding multiple threads and multiple trains of thought together, comics act as a sort of third-space—a place to let multiple stories and metaphors come together and interact. But more than a powerful tool for juxtapositions, comics are a place where the visual and the verbal exist side by side. In comics, the visual is equal partner to the verbal, not illustrative of the 'real' thing or mere decoration, but integral to thinking and sense-making.

Nick reflects. "I sought to offer a "fable for the future" that emphasizes this visual aspect in telling the story from a different angle. As I set forth to unravel what narrative inquiry meant and how best to present it, I was struck by the similarities between the process of doing narrative work as Ruth and Dave laid it out and life drawing. Unlike flat, snapshot models of research as "drive-by," narrative and life drawing convey the dynamic relationships between living beings in their uncertainties and their complexity. And from this starting point, and a lot of play in between, the following piece emerged.

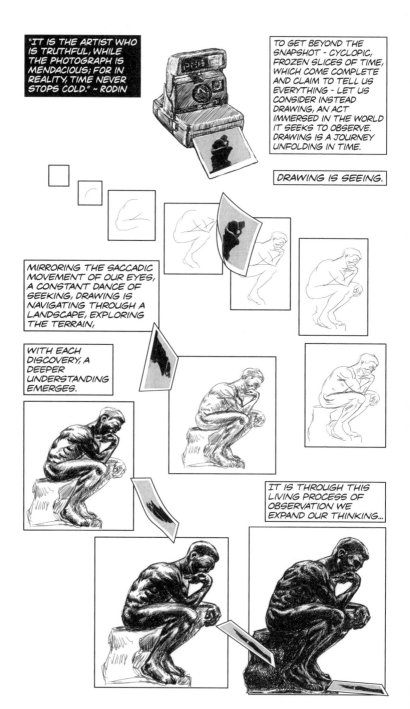

"IT IS THE ARTIST WHO IS TRUTHFUL, WHILE THE PHOTOGRAPH IS MENDACIOUS; FOR IN REALITY, TIME NEVER STOPS COLD." ~ RODIN

TO GET BEYOND THE SNAPSHOT - CYCLOPIC, FROZEN SLICES OF TIME, WHICH COME COMPLETE AND CLAIM TO TELL US EVERYTHING - LET US CONSIDER INSTEAD DRAWING, AN ACT IMMERSED IN THE WORLD IT SEEKS TO OBSERVE. DRAWING IS A JOURNEY UNFOLDING IN TIME.

DRAWING IS SEEING.

MIRRORING THE SACCADIC MOVEMENT OF OUR EYES, A CONSTANT DANCE OF SEEKING, DRAWING IS NAVIGATING THROUGH A LANDSCAPE, EXPLORING THE TERRAIN,

WITH EACH DISCOVERY, A DEEPER UNDERSTANDING EMERGES.

IT IS THROUGH THIS LIVING PROCESS OF OBSERVATION WE EXPAND OUR THINKING...

THE DISTANCE BETWEEN OUR EYES ITSELF MEANS THERE IS A DIFFERENCE BETWEEN THE VIEW EACH PRODUCES.

BY LOOKING ALTERNATELY THROUGH ONLY ONE EYE AT A TIME...

THIS DISPLACEMENT - PARALLAX - ENABLES US TO PERCEIVE DEPTH.

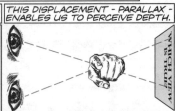

SIMILARLY, UTILIZING A TRIP HALFWAY AROUND THE SUN,

(MAKING TWO "EYES")

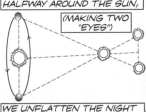

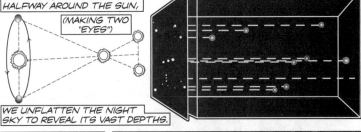

WE UNFLATTEN THE NIGHT SKY TO REVEAL ITS VAST DEPTHS.

JUST AS THE EARTH IS NO LONGER PERCEIVED AS THE CENTER OF THE UNIVERSE, THE DEPRIVILEGIZING OF A SINGLE ABSOLUTE VANTAGE POINT OPENS UP THE WORLD.

after Flammarion

IN ULYSSES, JOYCE EMPLOYED LITERARY PARALLAX VIA MULTIPLE NARRATORS TO EXPAND THE NARRATIVE'S DIMENSIONALITY. LIKE-WISE, MULTIPLE NARRATORS IN KUROSAWA'S RASHOMON DISPLACE NARRATIVE STABILITY AND DEMON-STRATE THAT THERE IS NO "TRUE" PERSPECTIVE.

BY MAKING OBSERVATIONS FROM MULTIPLE ANGLES,

WE CAN EXPAND OUR VISION...

125

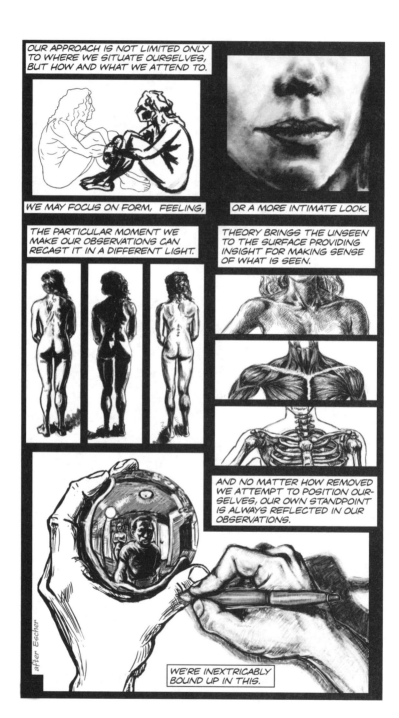

TAKEN TOGETHER, BAKHTIN SUGGESTS, THESE KALEIDOSCOPIC VIEWS OPEN OUR "OWN MONOLITHIC AND CLOSED WORLD" TO "THE GREAT WORLD OF ONE'S OWN PLUS 'THE OTHERS.'"

AND WHILE WE MAY FOLD AND STITCH THESE FRAGMENTS TOGETHER, THE ILLUSION OF SEAMLESSNESS IS ONLY THAT.

after Picasso

NUDE DECIDING A POSE

after Duchamp

EVEN THE MOST INFINITELY EXPANSIVE MAPPINGS, AS REBECCA SOLNIT WRITES, FAIL TO CAPTURE EVERYTHING, FOR "NO REPRESENTATION IS COMPLETE."

THERE ARE ALWAYS THINGS LEFT OUT - INDETERMINATE SPACES - GAPS; SITES OF POSSIBILITY AND EXPLORATION.

BOUNDED AND

BOUNDLESS...

after Mondrian

THE GAPS REMIND US THAT EVEN THIS -

- IN ALL ITS MULTIFACETED EXPANSIVENESS -

NOTES
R. Solnit, (p. 162)
A Field Guide to Getting Lost
M. Bakhtin, (p. 29)
The Dialogic Imagination

IS NOT THE FINAL WORD...

Mind the Gaps
by
NICK SOUSANIS
Thanks to Ruth & Dave for the opportunity, and to Leah for input & modeling

nsousanis@gmail.com

spinweaveandcut.com

127

References

Abu-Lughod, L. (1993). *Writing women's worlds: Bedouin stories*. Berkeley: University of California Press.

Addams, J. (1999). *Twenty years at Hull-House: With autobiographical notes*. New York: Signet.

Addams, J. (2002). *The long road of women's memory*. Chicago: University of Illinois Press.

Alexie, S. (2009). *The absolutely true diary of a part-time Indian*. New York: Little, Brown.

Altenbaugh, R. (1992). *The teacher's voice: A social history of teaching in twentieth-century America*. Washington, DC: Falmer.

Anzaldua, G. (2007). *Borderlands/la frontera: The new mestiza* (3rd ed.). San Francisco: Aunt Lute Books.

Ashley, C. (1944). *The Ashley book of knots*. New York: Doubleday.

Ashton-Warner, S. (1963). *Teacher*. New York: Touchstone.

Auster, P. (Ed.). (2001). *I thought my father was God and other true tales from NPR's National Story Project*. New York: Picador.

Bakhtin, M. (1981). *The dialogic imagination: Four essays* (M. Holquist, Ed.; C. Emerson & M. Holquist, Trans.). Austin: University of Texas Press.

Bal, M. (1997). *Narratology: Introduction to the theory of narrative* (C. van Boheemen, Trans.). London, ON: University of Toronto Press.

Barthes, R. (1977). *The rustle of language* (R. Howard, Trans.). Berkeley: University of California Press.

Bateson, C. (1994). *Peripheral visions: Learning along the way*. New York: HarperCollins.

Bechdel, A. (2007). *Fun home: A family tragicomic*. Seattle: Mariner.

Behar, R. (1994). *Translated woman: Crossing the border with Esperanza's story*. Boston: Beacon.

Behar, R. (1996). *The vulnerable observer: Anthropology that breaks your heart*. Boston: Beacon.

Belcher, D., & Connor, U. (Eds.). (2001). *Reflections on multi-literature lives*. Clevedon, England: Multilingual Matters.

Belenky, M., Clinchy, B., Goldberger, N., & Tarule, J. (1996). *Women's ways of knowing: The development of self, voice, and mind*. New York: Basic Books.

Bell, J. (1997). Teacher research in second and foreign language education. *Canadian Modern Language Review, 54*(1), 3-10.

Bell-Scott, P., & Johnson-Bailey, J. (1999). *Flat-footed truths: Telling black women's lives.* New York: Holt.

Berger, L. P., & Luckmann, T. (1967). *The social construction of reality: A treatise in the sociology of knowledge.* New York: Anchor.

Booth, W. (1983). *The rhetoric of fiction.* Chicago: University of Chicago Press.

Borges, J. (1969). *Ficciones.* New York: Grove Press.

Bourdieu, P., & Passeron, J. (1977). *Reproduction in education, society and culture.* London: Sage.

Britzman, D. (1991). *Practice makes practice: A critical study of learning to teach.* Albany: State University of New York Press.

Brown, K. M. (1991). *Mama Lola: A vodou priestess in Brooklyn.* Berkeley: University of California Press.

Bruner, E. M. (1989). *The anthropology of experience.* Urbana: University of Illinois Press.

Bruner, J. (1986). *Actual minds, possible worlds.* Cambridge, MA: Harvard University Press.

Bruner, J. (1991). The narrative construction of reality. *Critical Inquiry, 1,* 1–21.

Bruner, J. (2002). *Making stories: Law, literature, and life.* New York: Farrar, Straus, & Giroux.

Burroway, J. (2010). *Writing fiction: A guide to narrative craft* (8th ed.). New York: Longman.

Calvino, I. (1970). *If on a winter's night a traveler.* New York: Harcourt.

Carr, D. (1991). *Time, narrative, and history.* Bloomington: Indiana University Press.

Casanave, C. P., & Schecter, S. R. (Eds.). (1997). *On becoming a language educator: Personal essays on professional development.* Mahwah, NJ: Erlbaum.

Casey, K. (1993). *I answer with my life: Life histories of women teachers working for social change.* New York: Routledge.

Chatman, S. (1980). *Story and discourse: Narrative structure in fiction and film.* Ithaca, NY: Cornell University Press.

Clandinin, D. J. (2006). *Handbook of narrative inquiry.* Thousand Oaks, CA: Sage.

Clandinin, D. J., & Connelly, F. M. (2000). *Narrative inquiry: Experience and story in qualitative research.* San Francisco: Jossey-Bass.

Clandinin, D. J., & Connelly, F. M. (1990). *Narrative inquiry: Experience and story in qualitative research.* San Francisco: Jossey-Bass.

Clendinin, D., & Nagourney, A. (2001). *Out for good: The struggle to build a gay rights movement in America.* New York: Simon & Schuster.

Clifford, J., & Marcus, G. (1986). *Writing culture: The poetics and politics of ethnography.* Berkeley: University of California Press.

Clough, P. (2002). *Narratives and fictions in educational research.* Philadelphia: Open University Press.

Cobley, P. (2001). *Narrative.* New York: Routledge.

Cochran-Smith, M., & Lytle, S. (1992). *Inside/Outside: Teacher research and knowledge.* New York: Teachers College Press.

Cochran-Smith, M., & Lytle, S. (2009). *Inquiry as stance: Practitioner research in the next generation.* New York: Teachers College Press.

Cohan, S., & Shires, L. M. (1988). *Telling stories: A theoretical analysis of narrative fiction.* New York: Routledge.

Cohen, J. (1993). Constructing race at an urban high school: In their minds, their mouths, their hearts. In L. Weis & M. Fine (Eds.), *Beyond silenced voices: Class, race, and gender in United States schools* (pp. 289–323). Albany: State University of New York Press.

Cohler, B. J., & Hammach, P. L. (2006). Making a gay identity: Life story and the construction of a coherent self. In D. McAdams, R. Josselson, & A. Lieblich, (Eds.), *Identity and story: Creating self in narrative* (pp. 151-172). Washington, DC: American Psychological Association Press.

Coles, R. (1990). *The call of stories: Teaching and the moral imagination.* Cambridge, MA: Harvard University Press.

Collins, P. (1991). *Black feminist thought: Knowledge, consciousness and pedagogy.* Boston: Unwin Hyman.

Connelly, F. M., & Clandinin, D. J. (1990). Stories of experience and narrative inquiry. *Educational Researcher, 19*, 2–14.

Craib, I. (2004). Narratives as bad faith. In M. Andrews, S. D. Sclater, C. Squire, & A. Treacher (Eds.), *Uses of narrative* (pp. 64–74). Los Angeles: Transition.

Cross, B. (1996). *Sounding out the silences: Narratives and absences in African higher education* (Occasional Paper No. 59). Edinburgh: Edinburgh University, Centre for African Studies.

Cunliffe, A. L. (2003). Reflexive inquiry in organizational research: Questions and possibilities. *Human Relations, 56*(8), 983–1003.

Currie, M. (Ed.). (1995). *Metafiction.* New York: Longman.

Currie, M. (1998). *Postmodern narrative theory.* New York: Palgrave.

Daiute, C., & Lightfoot, C. (Eds.). (2004). *Narrative analysis: Studying the development of individuals in society.* Thousand Oaks, CA: Sage.

D'Emilio, J. (1998). *Intimate matters: A history of sexuality in America.* Chicago: University of Chicago Press.

Denzin, N. (1989). *Interpretive biography.* Newbury Park, CA: Sage.

Denzin, N. (1997). *Interpretive ethnography: Ethnographic practices for the 21st century.* Thousand Oaks, CA: Sage.

Destigter, T. (1998). The Tesoros Project: An experiment in democratic communities. *Research in the Teaching of English, 32*(1), 10–42.

Dewey, J. (1997a). *Democracy and education.* Boston: Free Press.

Dewey, J. (1997b). *Experience and education.* Boston: Free Press.

Dews, C. L. (1995). *This fine place so far from home: Voices of academics from the working class.* Philadelphia: Temple University Press.

Dickson, R. (1999). Confirming testimonies: Conversations with three women educators. (Doctoral dissertation, Teachers College, Columbia University, 1999). *Dissertation Abstracts International, 60-07,* 2450.

Docherty, T. (1996). The ethics of alterity: Postmodern carácter. In *Alterities: Criticism, history, representation* (pp. 36–68). Oxford: Clarendon Press.

Drooker, E. (2002). *Blood song: A silent ballad.* New York: Harcourt.

Duberman, M. (1994). *Stonewall.* New York: Penguin.

Dyson, A. (2002). Baktinian buzz about teacher talk: Discourse matters in "what difference does difference make?" *English Education, 35*(1), 6–20.

Dyson, A. H. (2003). *The brothers and sisters learn to write: Popular literacies in childhood and school culture.* New York: Teachers College Press.

Dyson, A., & Genishi, C. (2005). *On the case: Approaches to language and literacy research.* New York: Teachers College Press.

Eagleton, T. (2003). *The gatekeeper.* New York: St. Martin's Press.

Ely, M., Vinz, R., Anzul, M., & Downing, M. (1997). *On writing qualitative research: Living by words.* London: Falmer Press.

Erlich, V. (1980). *Russian formalism: History, doctrine.* Amsterdam: Mouton Press.

Farrell, E., Peguero, G., Lindsey, R., & White, R. (1988). Giving voice to high school students: Pressure and boredom, ya know what I'm sayin'? *American Educational Research Journal, 25,* 489–502.

Fecho, R. (2003). *Is this English? Race, language, and culture in the classroom.* New York: Teachers College Press.

Finn, P. (2009). *Literacy with an attitude: Educating working-class children in their own self-interest.* Albany: State University of New York Press.

Fleischer, C. (1995). *Composing teacher-research: A prosaic history.* Albany: State University of New York Press.

Florio-Ruane, S. (1991). Conversation and narrative in collaborative research: An ethnography of the written literacy forum. In C. Witherell & N. Noddings (Eds.), *Stories lives tell: Narrative and dialogue in education* (pp. 234–256). New York: Teachers College Press.

Fordham, S. (1988). Racelessness as a factor in black students' school success: Pragmatic strategy or pyrrhic victory? *Harvard Educational Review, 58,* 54–84.

Foster, M. (1997). *Black teachers on teaching.* New York: New Press.

Foucault, M. (1970) *The order of things: An archaeology of the human sciences.* New York: Vintage Books.

Fowler, L. C. (2006). *A curriculum of difficulty: Narrative research in education and the practice of teaching.* New York: Peter Lang.

Freeman, M. (1992). Self as narrative: The place of life history in studying the life span. In T. Brinthaupt & R. Lipka (Eds.), *The self: Definitional and methodological issues* (pp. 15–43). Albany: State University of New York Press.

Freeman, M. (1993). *Rewriting the self: History, memory, narrative.* London: Routledge.

Gallas, K. (1997). *Sometimes I can be anything: Power, gender and identity in a primary classroom.* New York: Teachers College Press.

Gallas, K. (2001). Look, Karen, I'm running like Jell-O: Imagination as a question, a topic, a tool for literacy research and learning. *Research in the Teaching of English, 35*(1), 457–492.

Geertz, C. (1983). *Local knowledge: Further essays in interpretive anthropology.* New York: Basic Books.

Geertz, C. (1998). *Works and lives: The anthropologist as author.* New York: Polity.

Genette, G. (1983). *Narrative discourse: An essay in method.* Ithaca, NY: Cornell University Press.

Gerard, P. (1998). *Creative nonfiction: Researching and crafting stories of real life.* New York: Writer's Digest.

Gilyard, K. (1991). *Voices of the self: A study of language competence.* Detroit: Wayne State University Press.

Giovanni, N. (1972). *My house.* New York: William Morrow.

Gitlin, A. (1992). *Teachers' voices for school change: An introduction to educative research.* New York: Teachers College Press.

Goodman, N. (1978). *Ways of worldmaking.* Indianapolis, IN: Hackett.

Gordon, E., McKibbin, K., Vasudevan, L., & Vinz, R. (2007). Writing out of the unexpected: Narrative inquiry and the weight of small moments. *English Education, 39*(4), 326–351.

Grealy, L. (2003). *Autobiography of a face.* New York: Harper.

Grumet, M. (1988). *Bitter milk: Women and teaching.* Amherst: University of Massachusetts Press.

Gubrium, J. F., & Holstein, J. A. (2009). *Analyzing narrative reality.* Thousand Oaks, CA: Sage.

Hardy, B. (1968). Towards a poetics of fiction: An approach through narrative. *Novel, 2,* 5–14.

Heller, J. (1997). *Something happened.* New York: Simon & Schuster.

Henry, A. (1998). *Taking back control: African Canadian women teachers' lives and practices.* New York: State University of New York Press.

Hicks, D. (2002). *Reading lives: Working-class children and literacy learning.* New York: Teachers College Press.

Hicks, D. (2004, August). Back to Oz? Or, rethinking the literacy in a critical study of reading. *Research and the Teaching of English, 39*(1), 63–84.

Hills, R. (2000). *Writing in general and the short story in particular.* Seattle: Mariner.

Hymes, D. (1972). Models of the interaction of language and social life. In J. Gumperz, (Ed.), *Directions in sociolinguistics: The ethography of communication* (pp. 35–71). New York: Holt, Rinehart & Winston.

Iser, W. (1993). *The fictive and the imaginary: Charting literary anthropology.* Baltimore: Johns Hopkins University Press.

Jakobson, R., Pomorska, K., & Rudy, S. (Eds.). (1990). *Language in literature.* Cambridge, MA: Belknap Press of Harvard University.

Jalongo, M. R., & Isenberg, J. P. (1995). *Teachers' stories: From personal narrative to professional insight.* San Francisco: Jossey-Bass.

Johnson-Bailey, J. (2000). *Sistahs in college: Making a way out of no way.* Malabar, FL: Krieger.

Joslin, K. (2004). *Jane Addams: A writer's life.* Urbana: University of Illinois.

Josselson, R. (1996). *Ethics and process in narrative study of lives.* Thousand Oaks, CA: Sage.

Josselson, R., & Lieblich, A. (Eds.). (1993). *The narrative study of lives* (Vol. 1). Thousand Oaks, CA: Sage.

Juzwik, M. M. (2006). Performing curriculum: Building ethos through narrative in pedagogical discourse. *Teachers College Record, 108*(4), 489–528.

Kellner, H. (1987). Narrativity in history: Post-structuralism and since. *History and Theory, 26,* 1–29.

Khan, S. (2010). Privilege: *The making of an adolescent elite at St. Paul's School.* Princeton, NJ: Princeton University Press.

Kooy, M. (2006). *Telling stories in book clubs: Women teachers and professional development.* New York: Springer.

Kozol, J. (1985). *Death at an early age.* New York: Plume. (Original work published 1967)

Kundera, M. (1988). *The book of laughter and forgetting.* New York: Harper.

Labov, W. (1972). The transformation of experience in narrative syntax. In W. Labov, (Ed.), *Language in the inner city* (pp. 354–396). Philadelphia: University of Pennsylvania Press.

Labov, W., & Waletzky, J. (1967). Narrative analysis. In J. Helm (Ed.), *Essays on the verbal and visual arts* (pp. 12– 44). Seattle: University of Washington Press.

Lacan, J. (1977). *Ecrits: A selection.* (A. Sheridan, Trans.). New York: Norton.

Lakoff, G., & Johnson, M. (1980). *Metaphors we live by.* Chicago: University of Chicago Press.

Lather, P. (1991). *Getting smart: Feminist pedagogy with/in the postmodern.* London: Routledge.

Lawrence-Lightfoot, S. (1985). *The good high school: Portraits of character and culture.* New York: Basic Books.

Lawrence-Lightfoot, S. (2003). *The essential conversation: What parents and teachers can learn from each other.* New York: Random House.

Lee, C. D., Rosenfeld, E., Mendenhall, R., Rivers, A., & Tynes, B. (2004). Cultural modeling as a frame for narrative analysis. In C. Daiute & C. Lightfoot (Eds.), *Narrative analysis: Studying the development of individuals in society* (pp. 39–62). Thousand Oaks, CA: Sage.

Lemon, L. T., & Reis, M. J. (Eds.). (1965). *Russian formalist criticism: Four essays.* Lincoln: University of Nebraska Press.

Levi-Strauss, C. (1967). *The scope of anthropology.* (S. O. Paul & R. A. Paul, Trans.). London: Cape.

Lieblich, A., Tuval-Mashiach, R., & Zilber, T. (1998). *Narrative research: Reading, analysis, and interpretation.* Thousand Oaks, CA: Sage.

Lightfoot, C. (2004). Fantastic self: A study of adolescents' fictional narratives, and aesthetic activity as identity work. In C. Daiute & C. Lightfoot (Eds.), *Narrative analysis: Studying the development of individuals in society* (pp. 21–37). Thousand Oaks, CA: Sage.

Linde, C. (1993). *Life stories: The creation of coherence.* New York: Oxford University Press.

Linklater, R., (Producer, Director). (1991). *Slacker* [Motion picture]. United States: Orion Classics.

Luttrell, W. (2003). *Pregnant bodies, fertile minds: Gender, race and the schooling of pregnant teens*. New York: Routledge.

Lyotard, J. (1984). *The postmodern condition: A report on knowledge: Vol. 10. Theory and history of literature* (G. Bennington & B. Massumi, Trans.). Minneapolis: University of Minnesota Press.

Martin, W. (2005). *The art of the short story*. New York: Wadsworth.

McInerney, J. (1997). *Bright lights, big city*. New York: Signet.

McQuillan, M. (Ed.). (2000). *The narrative reader*. New York: Routledge.

Measor, L., & Sikes, P. (1992). Visiting lives: Ethics and methodology in life history. In I. Goodson (Ed.), *Studying teachers' lives* (pp. 209–233). London: Routledge.

Meyer, R. (1996). *Stories from the heart: Teachers and students researching their literacy lives*. New York: Routledge.

Michaels, A. (1998). *Fugitive pieces*. New York: Random House.

Michie, G. (2009). *Holler if you hear me: The education of a teacher and his student*. New York: Teachers College Press.

Middleton, S. (1993). *Educating feminists: Life histories and pedagogy*. New York: Teachers College Press.

Mink, L. (1974). History and fiction as modes of comprehension. In R. Cohen (Ed.), *New directions in literary history* (pp. 107–124). Baltimore: Johns Hopkins Press.

Mitchell, W. J. T. (1981). *On narrative*. Chicago: University of Chicago Press.

Mohanty, C. (1991). *Feminism without borders: Decolonizing theory, practicing solidarity*. Durham, NC: Duke University Press.

Momaday, S. (1969). *The way to Rainy Mountain*. Santa Fe: University of New Mexico Press.

Moore, L. (2007). *Self help*. New York: Vintage Books.

Neilsen, L. (1998). Playing for real: Performative texts and adolescent identities. In D. E. Alvermann, K. A. Hinchman, D. W. Moore, S. F. Phelps, & D. R. Waff (Eds.), *Reconceptualizing literacies in adolescents' lives* (pp. 3–26). Mahwah, NJ: Erlbaum.

Oates, J. C. (2004). *The faith of a writer: Life, craft, art*. New York: Harper Perennial.

O'Brien, R. (Ed.). (2004). *Voices from the edge: Narratives about the Americans with Disabilities Act*. London: Oxford University Press.

O'Brien, T. (1990). *The things they carried*. New York: Penguin.

Ochberg, R. (2003). Teaching interpretation. In R. Josselson, A. Lieblich, & D. P. McAddams (Eds.), *Up close and personal: The teaching and learning of narrative research* (pp. 113–131). Washington, DC: American Psychological Association Press.

Ochs, E., & Capps, L. (2001). *Living narrative: Creating lives in everyday storytelling*. Cambridge, MA: Harvard University Press.

O'Connor, F. (1985). Preface. *The complete stories* (R. Giroux, Ed.). New York: Farrar, Straus, & Giroux.

Okri, B. (1997). *A way of being free*. London: Phoenix.

Ondaatje, M. (2004). *The collected works of Billy the Kid*. London: Bloomsbury.

Pagnucci, G. (2004). *Living the narrative life: Stories as a tool for meaning making*. Portsmouth, NH: Heinemann.

Paley, V. (1986). *Wally's stories*. Cambridge, MA: Harvard University Press.

Paley, V. (1990). *The boy who would be a helicopter: The uses of storytelling in the classroom*. Cambridge, MA: Harvard University Press.

Perl, S. (2005). *On Austrian soil: Teaching those I was taught to hate*. Albany: State University of New York Press.

Peters, M. A., & Burbules, N. C. (2004). *Poststructuralism and educational research*. New York: Rowman & Littlefield.

Plato. (1992). *Republic*. (G. M. Grub, Trans.). Indianapolis, IN: Hackett.

Plummer, K. (1995). *Telling sexual stories: Power, change, and social worlds*. New York: Routledge.

Polkinghorne, D. (1988). *Narrative knowing and the human sciences*. Albany: State University of New York Press.

Popular Memory Group. (1982). Popular memory: Theory, politics, method. In R. Johnson, G. McLennan, B. Schwartz, & D. Sutton (Eds.), *Making histories* (pp. 205–252). London: Hutchison.

Propp, V. (1968). *Morphology of the folktale* (L. Wagner, Ed.; L. Scott, Trans.). Austin: University of Texas Press.

Proust, M. (1982). *Remembrance of things past*. New York: Vintage Books.

Quantz, R. (1992). Interpretive method in historical research: Ethnohistory reconsidered. In R. Altenbaugh (Ed.), *The teacher's voice* (pp. 174–190). Washington, DC: Falmer.

Quinonez, E. (2000). *Bodega dreams*. New York: Vintage Books.

Quint, S. (1996). "Cause you talkin' about a whole person": A new path for schooling and literacy in troubled times and spaces. *Journal of Literacy Research, 28*, 310–319.

Rasmussen, D. (1995). Rethinking subjectivity: Narrative identity and the self. *Philosophy and Social Criticism, 21*(5), 159–172.

Reggio, G. (Director & Producer). (1982). *Koyaanisqatsi: Life out of balance* [Motion picture]. United States: MGM.

Richert, A. E. (2002). Narratives that teach: Learning about teaching from the stories teachers tell. In N. Lyons & V. LaBoskey (Eds.), *Narrative inquiry in practice advancing the knowledge of teaching* (pp. 48–62). New York: Teachers College Press.

Ricoeur, P. (1988). *Time and narrative* (Vol. III). Chicago: University of Chicago Press.

Riessman, C. (2008). *Narrative methods for the human sciences*. Thousand Oaks, CA: Sage.

Rimmon-Kenan, S. (1983). *Narrative fiction: Contemporary poetics*. London: Methuen.

Rodriguez, R. (2004). *Hunger of memory: The education of Richard Rodriguez*. New York: Dial Press.

Rogers, R. (Ed.). (2004). *An introduction to critical discourse analysis in education*. Mahwah, NJ: Erlbaum.

Rose, M. (2005). *Lives on the boundary: A moving account of the struggles and achievements of America's educationally underprepared*. New York: Penguin.

Rosenwald, G. C., & Ochberg, R. L. (Eds.). (1992). *Storied lives: The cultural politics of self-understanding*. New Haven, CT: Yale University Press.

Royster, J. J. (2000). *Traces of a stream: Literacy and social change among African American women*. Pittsburgh, PA: University of Pittsburgh Press.

Saks, A. L. (1996). Viewpoints: Should novels count as dissertations in education? *Research in the Teaching of English, 30*(4), 400–412.

Sandlin, J., & Clark, C. (2009). From opportunity to responsibility: Political master narratives, social policy, and success stories in adult literacy education. *Teachers College Record, 111*(4), 999–1029.

Sarbin, T. (Ed.). (1986). *Narrative psychology: The storied nature of human conduct.* Santa Barbara, CA: Praeger.

Schaafsma, D. (1993). *Eating on the street: Teaching literacy in a multicultural society.* Pittsburgh, PA: University of Pittsburgh Press.

Schmidt, J. (1998). *Women/writing/teaching.* Albany: State University of New York Press.

Shilts, R. (1987). *And the band played on: Politics, people, and the AIDS epidemic.* New York: St. Martin's Press.

Silko, L. M. (2006). *Ceremony.* New York: Penguin.

Singley, B. (2008). *When race becomes real: Black and white writers confront their personal histories.* Carbondale: Southern Illinois University Press.

Soltis, R. (2005). *A Field Guide to Getting Lost.* New York: Viking.

Spivak, G. (1999). *In other worlds: Essays in cultural politics.* New York: Routledge.

Stegner, W. (2002). *On teaching and writing fiction.* New York: Penguin.

Sterling, D. (1984). *We are your sisters: Black women in the nineteenth century.* New York: Norton.

Sterne, L. (2009). *The life and opinions of Tristram Shandy, gentleman.* Oxford: Oxford University Press. (Original work published 1759)

Stock, P. (1995). *The dialogic curriculum: Teaching and learning in a multicultural society.* Portsmouth, NH: Boynton/Cook.

Stronach, I., & MacLure, M. (1997). *Educational research undone: The postmodern embrace.* Philadelphia: Open University Press.

Taussig, M. (2004). *My cocaine museum.* Chicago: University of Chicago Press.

Todorov, T. (1981) *Introduction to poetics* (R. Howard, Trans.). Minneapolis: University of Minnesota.

Trimmer, J. (1997). *Narration as knowledge: Tales of the teaching life.* Portsmouth, NH: Boynton/Cook.

Van Maanen, J. (1988). *Tales of the field: On writing ethnography.* Thousand Oaks, CA: Sage.

Vielstimmig, M. (1999). Petals on a wet, black bough: Textuality, collaboration, and the new essay. In G. Hawisher and C. Selfe (Eds.), *Passions, Pedagogies, and 21st Century Technologies* (pp. 89-114). Logan: Utah State University Press.

Villaneuva, V. (1993). *Bootstraps: From an American academic of color.* Urbana, IL: National Council of Teachers of English.

Vinz, R. (1996). *Composing a teaching life.* Portsmouth, NH: Boynton/Cook.

Vonnegut, K. (1998). *Cat's cradle.* New York: Dell.

Vygotsky, L. (1978). *Mind in society* (M. Cole, V. John-Steiner, S. Schribner, & E. Souberman, Eds.; A. Luria, M. Lopez-Morillas, & M. Cole, Trans.). Cambridge, MA: Harvard University Press.

Walker, V. S. (2005). Organized resistance and black educators' quest for school equality, 1878–1938. *Teachers College Record, 107,* 355–388.

Walkerdine, V. (1991). *Schoolgirl fictions.* London: Verso.

Webster, L., & Mertova, P. (2007). *Using narrative inquiry as a research method: An introduction to using critical event narrative analysis in research on learning and teaching.* New York: Routledge.

Weiler, K. (1988). *Women teaching for change: Gender, class and power.* South Hadley, MA: Bergin & Garvey.

Weiler, K. (1992). Remembering and representing life choices: A critical perspective on teachers' oral history narratives. *Qualitative Studies in Education, 5,* 39–50.

Weiner Katz, W. J., & Rosenwald, G. J. (1993). A moment's monument: The psychology of keeping a diary. In R. Josselson & A. Lieblich (Eds.), *The narrative study of lives* (Vol. 1). Thousand Oaks, CA: Sage.

Weis, L., & Fine, M. (Eds.). (1993). *Beyond silenced voices: Class, race, and gender in United States schools.* Albany: State University of New York Press.

White, H. (1987). *The content of the form: Narrative discourse and historical representation.* Baltimore: Johns Hopkins Press.

Willis, G., & Schubert, W. (1991). *Reflections from the heart of educational inquiry: Understanding curriculum and teaching through the arts.* Troy, NY: Educators International Press.

Winterson, J. (1995). *Art Objects.* London: Jonathan Cape.

Witherell, C., & Noddings, N. (Eds.). (1991). *Stories lives tell: Narrative and dialogue in education.* New York: Teachers College Press.

Wolf, M. (1992). *A thrice told tale: Feminism, postmodernism, and ethnographic responsibility.* Palo Alto, CA: Stanford University Press.

Woolf, V. (2008). *Mrs. Dalloway.* London: Oxford University Press.

Yang, G. (2005). *American born Chinese.* Seattle: Square Fish Press.

Index

About the Authors

Sara Brock teaches English at a public high school on Long Island, NY. She recently completed her doctorate at Teachers College, where she received the Walter Sindlinger Writing Award. In her dissertation, she explored the influence of fairy tales, quest novels, and other literary genres on narratives of teaching and learning.

Randi Dickson is Assistant Professor and co-director of English Education at Queens College/CUNY. She worked as an English and Writing Center Director in secondary public schools for 20 years. She has articles in *English Education, English Journal, Voices from the Middle, and Language Arts*.

David Schaafsma is an Associate Professor of English and Director of English Education at the University of Illinois at Chicago. He is a former high school English teacher and co-editor, with Ruth, of *English Education*. David is the author of *Eating on the Street: Teaching Literacy in a Multicultural Society* and co-author of *Language and Reflection: An Integrated Approach to Teaching Literacy*, which was awarded the CEE Richard Meade Award for Outstanding Research in English Education.

Nick Sousanis is a doctoral candidate at Teachers College, Columbia University. His dissertation on "unflattening," explores curiosity in learning through comic book format. Sousanis is the biographer of legendary Detroit artist Charles McGee. Samples of his educational comics can be seen at www.spinweaveandcut.com/.

Ruth Vinz is a Professor in English Education and the Enid and Lester Morse Endowed Professor in Teacher Education at Teachers College, Columbia University. She has authored 13 books, and numerous articles and book chapters on teacher knowledge, literature education, and narratives of teacher learning. Her book, *Composing a Teaching Life*, received the CEE Richard Meade Award for Outstanding Research in English Education.